net
gain

net gain

expanding
markets through
virtual communities

John Hagel III
Arthur G. Armstrong

HARVARD BUSINESS SCHOOL PRESS
BOSTON, MASSACHUSETTS

Copyright © 1997 by McKinsey & Company, Inc.

All rights reserved

Printed in the United States of America

01 00 99 98 97   5 4 3 2 1

Library of Congress Cataloging-in-Publication Data

Hagel, John.
  Net gain: expanding markets through virtual communities / John
Hagel III, Arthur Armstrong.
      p.   cm.
  Includes index.
  ISBN 0-87584-759-5 (alk. paper)
  1. Internet marketing.   2. Customer relations.   I. Armstrong,
Arthur.   II. Title.
  HF5415.1265.H34   1997
  658.8'00285'467—dc 20   96-41597
                                                                 CIP

*The paper used in this publication meets the requirements of the American National
Standard for Permanence of Paper for Printed Library Materials Z39.49-1984.*

*We dedicate this book, with love, to Jane, Rebecca, and Rachel,
and to Kathy and Emily, whose contribution to this endeavor was
their unflagging encouragement and the time we would have otherwise
spent with them.*

*"One man gives freely yet gains even more. Another withholds unduly,
but comes to poverty."*

Proverbs 11:24

contents

preface   ix

PART I

the real value of virtual communities |

chapter 1   the race belongs to the swift   2

chapter 2   reversing markets: *how customers gain*   16

chapter 3   the new economics of virtual communities   41

chapter 4   the shape of things to come   82

PART II

building a virtual community |

chapter 5   choosing the way in   112

chapter 6   laying the foundation: *getting to critical mass*   131

chapter 7   the gardener's touch: *managing organic growth*   150

chapter 8   equipping the community: *choosing the right technology*   171

PART III

positioning to win the broader game |

chapter 9   rethinking functional management   186

chapter 10   reshaping markets and organizations   203

management agenda   217

further reading   221

index   225

about the authors   235

preface

OUR INTEREST IN VIRTUAL COMMUNITIES has evolved over many years—a veritable eternity in "Net" time. It began in the late 1980s, when we observed the emergence and growth of The Well, a vibrant, engaging on-line community of leading-edge thinkers at the intersection of technological and cultural change. The focus on bulletin boards and e-mail within The Well drove home the message that networks are ultimately about the connections they create between people. It also underscored the importance of a new form of content generated by The Well's members as they interacted on-line. Over time, the accumulated postings to the bulletin boards in The Well became a treasure trove of information that drew in more people and led them, in turn, to comment on and contribute to the community's cumulative knowledge.

Through The Well, we also became aware of a vast, highly fragmented underground culture of independent bulletin boards operating via the telephone network. Established and maintained—usually on a part-time basis in a spare bedroom or garage—by people passionate about a particular topic, these bulletin boards had become on-line gathering places for others who shared their interest. Sports, role-playing games, diabetes, gun collecting, plumbing supplies, politics, relationships, stock investments—the range of topics appeared endless. Thousands of such bulletin boards were in existence, and although most involved mere hundreds of members, in aggregate they were drawing in millions of domestic and international participants.

Most of these initiatives were motivated by passion, not profit. In fact, there was a strong anticommerce culture in the on-line world and particularly on the Internet, at that time a relatively new network platform hosting a broad range of "news groups" that brought people together around topics of common interest. The profit motive was almost entirely absent until the emergence of commercial on-line services like Prodigy, America Online, and CompuServe. The success of America Online and CompuServe, with their emphasis on bulletin boards and chat, relative to Prodigy, with its focus on "broadcasting" published content, once again highlighted the importance of connections among people.

The second impetus for this book came from our work with clients at McKinsey & Company. Many of them—from a broad range of industries, including media, telecommunications, health care, and financial services—had begun offering content and services on the network, expecting to develop new markets. In working with these clients, we soon discovered that the key to exploiting the new market opportunity in on-line networks was through combining content and communication. Virtual communities provided a powerful context for this integration and were therefore more than just an interesting social phenomenon. In fact, they were the kernel of a fundamentally new business model.

Our perspectives were also shaped by McKinsey's work in helping clients wrestle with the business implications of multimedia technologies. By providing richer experiences for users, and by enabling new forms of commercial activity, multimedia technologies are transforming electronic networks. In working with our clients, we began to envision the emergence of entirely new businesses, based wholly on these multimedia-enabled networks, that could offer significantly greater value to their customers than could businesses still operating within the bricks and mortar of physical space. Of course, virtual communities are not emerging in a vacuum. They will be influenced by many other elements of today's changing environment, such as multiple technology discontinuities and the liberalization and deregulation of trade, that demand new approaches to strategy and organization, including Web strategies, scenario management, evolutionary modeling, and the capability to "cannibalize" a company's own existing businesses.

We decided to write this book in order to draw wide attention to the virtual community business model, which we believe will become a central feature on the business landscape of the next decade. We seek to reach many diverse audiences. First and foremost, we are speaking to those who aspire to build their own virtual communities, particularly to the senior management of large companies capable of embracing the new model and creating value and customer relationships on a much broader plane than even the most ambitious management has imagined. We also want to reach those creative entrepreneurs who have already ventured out onto the network and who, in a variety of ways, are experimenting with elements of the new business model. Many of them are close to realizing the full power of this new business model, but, as we will argue in the book, no one has yet cracked the code and harnessed this power. More broadly, we want to address the general public, especially those who have detected a glimmer of some very new possibilities in the growth of electronic networks, but who are not yet sure what it means for their professional or personal lives.

We want to be clear about our intentions. We want to provide all of our readers with an understanding of this new business model as a way to help them navigate the challenges of establishing and managing a virtual community as a commercial enterprise. To paraphrase a prominent philosopher of social change, we are not seeking to interpret this new world—our goal is to help change it.

Because we're not pursuing understanding as an end in its own right, we have not embarked on an extended description and analysis of virtual community initiatives. Nor have we attempted to provide a detailed "how-to" manual on community formation, which would be premature at this stage. Instead, we focus on basic principles of successful community development that will help unleash the creativity and innovation required to explore and to exploit the enormous potential embedded in the virtual community concept.

It should also be clear that we are discussing virtual communities as a commercial enterprise. Howard Rheingold and others have insightfully described communities that exist as a purely social phenomenon. Some of these observers believe that virtual communities are antithetical to commerce. Our view is that the profit motive will in fact create new forms of virtual communities whose strong commercial element will enhance and expand the basic requirements of community—trust and commitment to each other.

Finally, we should acknowledge three inevitable limitations in writing this book. The first arises from the profound uncertainties associated with evolving electronic networks and the myriad business models emerging in the primordial brew known as cyberspace. At one level, the only thing we know for sure is that the evolution of this new environment will surprise us all. At another level, we have convictions about certain likely directions of evolution. We have made our assumptions explicit so that readers can test and evaluate them.

Second, the need to be concise has led us to make some generalizations about the likely evolution of virtual communities and the key principles for success. As with all generalizations, these have their inevitable exceptions and refinements when applied to specific situations. Generalizations are useful to orient the reader and to simplify a very confusing landscape but dangerous if mechanically applied in all situations. As we will describe, a rich variety of virtual communities is likely to evolve, differentiated by focus, membership, economics, cultural roots, and time of formation. Every community will be unique and will require its own set of strategies and organization to succeed.

Third, we do not expect virtual communities to be the only "form of life" on public networks. Indeed, many other commercial and noncommercial formats (including directories, market spaces, "web 'zines," corporate sites, and game areas) will thrive on these networks as well. But given the need for focus, and our belief that virtual communities will be the most competitive commercial on-line format, we have chosen to concentrate exclusively on this format.

To guide readers through this unfamiliar landscape, we have organized *Net Gain* into three parts. The first, "The Real Value of Virtual Communities," describes the power and potential of the virtual community concept. It begins with an overview of the key perspectives presented in the book and goes on to describe virtual communities in more detail—their role in shifting economic value from vendors to customers, their potential for value creation as based on the dynamics of increasing returns, and their likely evolution through a series of distinct stages.

With this context in place, the second part, "Building a Virtual Community," focuses on entering this new business. It discusses targeting the kind of community to start up; the principles of a successful entry strategy, emphasizing the need to generate, engage, and lock in traffic over time; understanding the distinctive characteristics of community organization; and selecting the right technology.

The third and final part, "Positioning to Win the Broader Game," pulls back from the virtual community itself to discuss the fundamental ways in which the emergence and spread of virtual communities will alter traditional business. We argue that traditional business functions—especially those in direct contact with the customer, such as marketing and sales—will be significantly transformed in a community environment. More broadly, we anticipate that virtual communities will reshape both traditional industry structures and business organizations. Virtual communities are not an opportunity that executives can choose to address or to ignore. They represent a profound change that will unalterably transform the business landscape—and benefit only those who confront it head on.

ACKNOWLEDGMENTS

In the course of writing this book, we have benefited from an enormous amount of help from a broad range of sources. Our greatest learning has come from working with our clients, who kept us focused and action-oriented in an area that all too easily inspires speculation and abstraction. In keeping with our policies of client confidentiality, we cannot acknowledge the help and encouragement we have received from individual clients and client executives, but we certainly wish to express our gratitude for the opportunity to test and refine our perspectives in so many different environments, both in the United States and around the world.

Within McKinsey & Company, our colleagues and partners have supported and contributed to our effort. We are especially indebted to the Multimedia Practice leadership—Ennius Bergsma, Sanjeev Dheer, Lorraine Harrington, Conor Kehoe, Nicholas Lovegrove, Takashi Nawa, Mike Nevens, Greg Reed, John Rose, Paul Sagawa, Chuck Stucki, Dennis Sweeney, and Michael Wilshire. In countless client and internal workshops, we have worked together to integrate and synthesize a perspective on the multimedia landscape that has provided a strong foundation for writing this book. In particular, we offer our thanks to Mike Nevens, who tirelessly read each iteration of the manuscript and contributed detailed comments and suggestions for improvement. We also acknowledge the help of members of the leadership group who have now left McKinsey and are applying some of these concepts in their own enterprises—Chip Austin, Richard Blue, Willy Burkhardt, Tom Eisenmann, Thomas Hesse, and Will Lansing.

We have also been helped by many others in the Multimedia Practice who have seen the power and potential of the virtual community concept and contributed to sharpening the perspective presented in this book. Shayne McQuade contributed above and beyond the call of duty in developing a computer-based business dynamics model that helped to quantify the enormous economic potential underlying the virtual community concept. Ably supported by Amy Eisner, Nick Hoffman, and Soo Kim, Shayne worked closely with, and benefited from the insight of, Corey Peck from High Performance Systems, the company that developed the modeling software. We would like to thank our colleagues who contributed their perspectives after roaming through various regions of the on-line world, including Neil Platt, Mina Muraki, Shengaza DaSent, Kevin Charlton, and Einat Wilf. We also owe a debt of gratitude to Joanna Barsh, Roy Berggren, Sameer Chisty, Justin Colledge, Jed Dempsey, Bob Dennis, Jon Garcia, Raj Garg, Ralph Heck, Masao Hirano, Detlev Hoch, Kristina Isakovitch, David Katz, Rich Koppel, Rod Laird, Mark Leiter, Brook Manville, Alan Miles, Finn Persson, Nina Pustilnik, Rob Rosiello, Toni Sacconaghi, Jack Stephenson, Somu Subramaniam, Anders Thulin, Luis Ubinas, Shinichi Ueyama, Kunihiko Yogo, and Michael Zeisser, all of whom shared their experiences and insights on electronic commerce and virtual communities.

We received significant support from the Business Dynamics Practice in helping to design the economic model for virtual communities. In particular, Glenn Cornett, Andrew Doman, Olivier Sibony, and Jayant Sinha provided valuable insight and suggestions.

This book benefited, too, from the unstinting help and editorial guidance of Lang Davison, of the firm's Communications Group. Lang worked with us throughout the writing process to sharpen our message, tighten our structure, and prune out secondary material. We would also like to thank Partha Bose and the editors of *The McKinsey Quarterly* for providing a forum and strong encouragement for some of the concepts in this book. Gene Zelazny and David Wentworth developed creative illustrations and exhibits under tight deadlines, and helped us clarify many of our more abstract points. Linda Kraemer and Greg Prang helped to gather material for the book, providing examples to illustrate key points. Our faithful assistants, Carrie Howell and Rosemary Garcia, cheerfully provided support during evenings and weekends to ensure that our manuscript met deadlines.

Outside McKinsey, we have drawn on the experience of many brave entrepreneurs who are pioneering the virtual community field. Peter Friedman, Jenna Woodul, and Bernard Bernstein of LiveWorld

Productions; John Borthwick, Janice Gjertsen, and Ted Werth of Total New York; Jerry Michalski of Release 1.0; Mason Myers and Kevin Watters of The Main Quad; Nick Grouf and Salman Malik of Agents, Inc.; Scott Murphy of Small World Software; and Greg Johnson of Magnet Interactive Studio—each provided valuable input to our thinking. Jeffrey Rayport and David Yoffie at the Harvard Business School have also helped to shape our thinking in key areas. Brian Arthur and Stuart Kauffman at the Santa Fe Institute provided a broader theoretical perspective on increasing returns and the behavior and evolution of complex adaptive systems that has profoundly influenced how we approach highly uncertain business environments.

Last, but clearly not least, we would like to express our appreciation to our colleagues at the Harvard Business School Press, at whose instigation we embarked on this project, and whose input, responsiveness, and support were crucial to its successful completion. In particular we would like to thank Nick Philipson, our editor, whose perceptive insights helped focus our message at each stage of the manuscript's development; Barbara Roth, who patiently shepherded the book through an accelerated production schedule; Carol Franco, director of the Press; and their colleagues Chuck Dresner, Sarah McConville, Gayle Treadwell, and Leslie Zheutlin. We are also very grateful to Tom Kiely, our editor at the *Harvard Business Review*, at whose initiative the idea of a book around this topic was first considered.

Needless to say, we have chosen to venture out on a very long limb in speculating on the direction and potential for virtual communities. The perspective and points of view expressed in this book, although shaped by many people and influences, are ultimately our own. We eagerly anticipate having company on the limb, but, for now, we are willing to test its strength on our own. Whatever the consequences, the view is energizing.

I

the real **value** of
virtual communities

1

the race
belongs
to the swift

The rise of virtual communities in
on-line networks has set in motion an
unprecedented shift in power from vendors
of goods and services to the customers
who buy them. Vendors who understand
this transfer of power and choose to
capitalize on it by organizing virtual
communities will be richly rewarded with
both peerless customer loyalty and
impressive economic returns. But the race
to establish the virtual community belongs
to the swift: those who move quickly and
aggressively will gain—and likely hold—
the advantage.

COMMERCIAL ENTERPRISES ARE RELATIVE newcomers to the on-line world, and so far few of them have made money there. Most businesses on the Internet and other networks today do little more than advertise their wares on "billboards" on the World Wide Web in the hope that a passing surfer will stop long enough to buy something. These old-media advertisements, dressed in their new-media clothes, are only one indication that marketers have yet to discover the secret to unlocking the revolutionary potential of the Internet and other networks.

Like every communications network, the Internet is all about establishing and reinforcing connections between people. This is a lesson that Alexander Graham Bell, whose invention grew into the biggest and best known of today's communications networks, long resisted. Bell was convinced that the primary value of his new device would be to deliver news reports and symphonies to the people. It wasn't until after he was presented with undeniable evidence that he conceded the primary use of the telephone was for people to communicate with each other.

> *Bell had to be convinced the best use of the telephone was for people to communicate.*

Television was also misperceived in its early years, when it was seen as little more than a medium for stage plays. Early broadcasts simply placed a microphone at the edge of the stage and pointed the camera toward the actors. Advertisements consisted of slightly reconfigured radio ads. Only later did advertisers and programmers realize the medium not only allowed but called for new approaches. The Internet today is at a parallel stage in which advertisers and content providers have yet to develop marketing and content that leverages the innate capabilities of the medium. *[Authors' note: This book covers the growth of virtual communities on all electronic networks. The Internet is probably the best known, but far from the only, electronic network operating today. Commercial on-line services like America Online, and private networks like funds-transfer networks for banks and bulletin board services using the telephone network, are all platforms for virtual communities. Because the Internet increasingly provides the connective tissue that links all of these other networks, we will refer to the Internet as a generic network platform unless otherwise indicated.]* Since the early 1970s, scientists have used the Internet and its predecessors to share data, collaborate on research, and exchange messages. In essence, scientists formed interactive research communities that existed not on a physical campus but on the Internet. These were the first virtual communities.

Since then, the reach of the Internet has expanded exponentially. More than 30 million computer users worldwide had access the World Wide Web as of 1996, and this number will increase to well over 100 million by the end of the decade. Commercial on-line services such as Prodigy, CompuServe, and America Online provided network access and specialized content and communication services to more than 10 million computer users in 1996. A broad subculture has emerged around thousands of fragmented bulletin board services, resulting in the creation of virtual communities that leverage the capabilities of the network to connect people with each other and to fulfill their specific needs for communication, information, and entertainment. One of the earliest and most robust of these virtual communities is The Well, launched in 1985 by a group of high-tech enthusiasts in northern California. Over the past decade, more than 10,000 computer users have communicated with each other through The Well, and many have developed personal relationships on-line and off.

Meanwhile, such diverse vendors as flower distributors, booksellers, liquor companies, and manufacturers of durable goods have rushed to develop sites on the World Wide Web where visitors can obtain information about the company and its products and send electronic messages. Some of the more sophisticated commercial sites allow visitors to play games and order products electronically. But rarely do these sites encourage communication between visitors to the site. (Most existing communities, such as The Well, are not business oriented; in fact, most strongly oppose the very idea of commercial activity on the Internet.)

By adapting to the culture of these networks, however, and by giving customers the ability to interact with each other as well as with the company itself, businesses can build new and deeper relationships with customers. We believe that commercial success in the on-line arena will belong to those who organize virtual communities to meet multiple social and commercial needs. By creating strong virtual communities, businesses will be able to build membership audiences and use those audiences to bring in revenues in the form of advertising, transaction fees, and membership fees.

Net Gain is designed to inform the senior management of large companies and entrepreneurs alike about the power of virtual communities to create value in on-line markets. We believe the time is right for addressing this commercial potential. The necessary network and computing technology infrastructure is now practically in place.

In the United States, at least, PCs are widely deployed in both the workplace and at home. As modem speeds have increased and higher bandwidth options (such as ISDN and cable modems) have been deployed, the ability to deliver reasonable graphics content over networks has been established. Support services such as billing systems, directories, and payment mechanisms are now being established. And a substantial share of the population is now not only computer literate but also experienced in communicating and accessing data over digital networks. In fact, the demographic profile of on-line users in the United States is rapidly converging with the overall demographics of the population.

Taken together, these factors indicate that businesses can leverage a broad and rich technology infrastructure and a sophisticated user base in the process of building virtual communities. Since the incremental investment that each must make to build a virtual community is small relative to the accumulated investment represented by this infrastructure, the Internet quite literally allows virtual community organizers to leverage the prior investments of others. *[Authors' note: Throughout the book we refer to virtual community organizers inclusively— whether they are start-ups established for the purpose of organizing a community or Global 500 giants expanding into the virtual community world from their primary lines of business.]* While this infrastructure is most broadly deployed in the United States, other countries are rapidly investing to build comparable capabilities. In the meantime, the Internet can now be accessed from any place in the world (at least from any place that has a telephone). Thus, leading-edge users in other countries have the ability and incentive to "get connected," which has led to the rapid proliferation of the Internet in such areas as Scandinavia and Australia.

Some readers may argue that the Internet is not yet ready to meet the needs of their particular industry or market. Others may believe that the commercial potential of electronic commerce is unproven. Such skepticism is understandable given that as yet few businesses have discovered how to generate traffic at a Web site, let alone how to do business with customers when they get there or how to gather the kind of information from those customers that will interest other advertisers and vendors in participating in the site. These skeptics might argue that it won't be worthwhile competing on electronic networks until the economic model is more proven.

Understandable as their doubts may be, we suspect such skeptics have yet to understand fully or take into account the laws of increasing returns and the ways in which they're changing the rules of the game in manufacturing, service, and knowledge-based industries. Until Bill Gates and his fellow shareholders made a killing at Microsoft, increasing returns were thought to exist only in textbooks. Now their existence in high-tech markets (like software and multimedia) and even in lower-tech industries (like retailing, banking, and insurance) is widely acknowledged.

As Microsoft proved most spectacularly, harnessing the power of increasing returns means "the more you sell, the more you sell." Microsoft saw and exploited the increasing returns potential of business webs—the idea that the more people participate in the business web, the more valuable the web becomes. In this case, the business web was the array of companies designing products based on the Microsoft operating system standard. The more companies that joined this web, the more useful the entire web became to computer buyers and the more units of the operating system Microsoft sold. Figure 1-1 shows the exponential growth of Microsoft revenues after a slow ramp-up period as it built its "web" of users.

Of course, the converse is also true: increasing returns make it all the more likely, if you are on the losing end in a market, that you will fall farther behind. That's why preemptive strategies become so important in markets where increasing returns prevail—if you don't get there first, you may be too late. As the saying goes in Silicon Valley, "Speed is God, and time is the devil."

The advantages of being among the first make the most compelling argument for beginning to plan for a virtual community now. Once the market really begins to take off, it will become increasingly difficult (and expensive) to catch up with market leaders. But we're also mindful of

"Speed is God, and time is the devil."

the various levels of uncertainty that substantially increase risk for those who move quickly. Specifically, this risk results from the uncertainty concerning how virtual communities will evolve over time, where value creation will concentrate, and what technologies will emerge that can enhance commercial activity on the Internet. Balancing this uncertainty with the urgency that's the result of powerful increasing returns dynamics will not be easy, but those who adopt leveraged strategies and rely wherever possible on the resources of others to build their community will both reduce risk and speed up community development.

WHO BENEFITS FROM VIRTUAL COMMUNITIES AND WHY

The benefits of the virtual community go to both customer and vendor. The benefits to customers flow from the very characteristics that

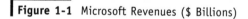

Figure 1-1 Microsoft Revenues ($ Billions)

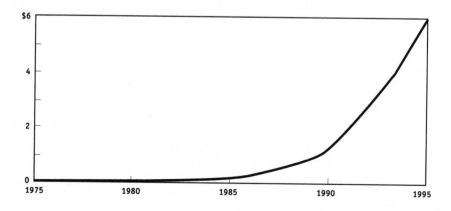

define a virtual community. The benefits to vendors have to do with new opportunities to expand their markets.

Power to the customer

Virtual communities have the power to reorder greatly the relationship between companies and their customers. Put simply, this is because they use networks like the Internet to enable customers to take control of their own value as potential purchasers of products and services. Today customers realize very little of the value their demographic information and transaction histories represent. Direct mail companies, for instance, pay large sums for lists of customers to whom they can market. Magazines and credit-card companies "rent" out their subscriber and cardholder lists to nearly any company interested in trying to sell to these customers. But customers themselves capture very little of the economic value their own information creates. In contrast, two of the largest retailers of mailing lists for the U.S. direct marketing industry, American List Corporation and American Business Information, enjoy market capitalization of more than $8 billion and $4 billion, respectively.

This will change as customers become more sophisticated capturers and managers of their own information. Virtual communities will play an essential role in this process by organizing and orchestrating the information and transaction capabilities that will allow customers to extract ever more value from the vendors they interact with. In essence, virtual communities will act as agents for their members by helping them to get increased product and service information—not to mention lower prices—from vendors at the same time that they meet a broad range of social needs to communicate.

Five defining elements of the virtual community business model combine to deliver this powerful value proposition:

1. **Distinctive focus:** Virtual communities are identified by a specific focus, to help potential members readily understand what kind of resources they are likely to find there and to help community organizers determine the full range of resources likely to be required to meet members' needs. For example, the focus may be on a geographic area (say, Atlanta or Paris), a topical area (sports or foreign affairs), a vertical industry (law firms or plumbing supply manufacturers), or functional expertise (market research or purchasing management).

2. ***Capacity to integrate content and communication:*** Virtual communities provide a broad range of published content (including, where appropriate, advertisements and vendor information) consistent with the distinctive focus of the community, and they integrate this content with a rich environment for communication. Communication capability—through bulletin boards on which members can "post" messages accessible to all, chat areas where real-time written "conversations" are conducted, and e-mail—allows members to maximize the value of this content, enabling them to clarify their understanding of the content by communicating with its publisher and to evaluate the credibility of the content by communicating with each other.

3. ***Appreciation of member-generated content:*** In addition to published content, virtual communities provide environments for the generation and dissemination of member-generated content. This is perhaps the single most empowering element of a virtual community. It gives members the capability to compare and aggregate their experiences, which in turn creates for them a fuller range of information and a perspective independent of vendors and advertisers on the resources that are important to the members.

4. ***Access to competing publishers and vendors:*** Virtual communities are organizing agents for their members. As such, they will seek to aggregate the broadest range of high-quality resources possible, including competing publishers and vendors, and to maximize the information and product options available so that their members can make more informed, cost-effective decisions on what resources they need.

5. ***Commercial orientation:*** Virtual communities will increasingly be organized as commercial enterprises, with the objective of earning an attractive financial return by providing members with valuable resources and environments through which to enhance their own power. It is precisely this profit incentive that will shape the evolution of virtual communities as vehicles to augment the power of their members. Members will value this power and richly reward the community organizers that deliver it to them most effectively, abandoning those which compromise on this value proposition. It is in giving a net gain in value to their members that community organizers will realize a substantial net gain of their own. Of course, many of the early examples of virtual communities involve

noncommercial (one might even say anticommercial) initiatives, but our focus will be on the commercial potential of this new system for organizing resources on the network.

It's clear that the virtual community organizer must focus on two imperatives to deliver the value proposition: aggregating members and aggregating resources relevant to members. These two imperatives in turn suggest a third imperative: aggregating information profiles about members' use of the network and the transactions they carry out on the network. By aggregating such profiles, community organizers can develop a better understanding of the needs of their members and thereby become more effective in aggregating the right resources. In subsequent chapters we will explore the ways in which community organizers can deliver what these three imperatives demand.

Profit to the vendor

Customers aren't the only ones who stand to benefit from virtual communities. Vendors (which throughout the book we define as the companies that produce, sell, and/or distribute goods and services) will find in the virtual community a powerful vehicle for expanding their markets— as long as they don't let competitors or an independent third party beat them to the punch by capturing the primary loyalty of their customers.

If you don't convert your customers to virtual communities, someone else will do it for you.

Virtual communities help vendors expand their markets on two levels: through capabilities that are unique to the virtual community business model and through capabilities that are more broadly available in network-based environments. Elements specific to virtual communities that help vendors expand their markets include the following.

- *Reduced search costs:* Vendors and customers can find each other more easily because virtual communities provide an environment for aggregating relevant participants and information about those participants.

- *Increased propensity for customers to buy:* Customers perceive less risk and experience more excitement. By aggregating a broad range of information and options for its members, community organizers help to reduce the perceived risk of purchase. By providing an engaging environment where members interact with each other, as well as with vendors, excitement around "hot" products can be quickly generated.

- **Enhanced ability to target:** Virtual communities will accumulate detailed profiles of members and their transaction histories, not only with a single vendor but with multiple vendors across an entire product category. As we will explain later in the book, ownership of these profiles is likely to shift over time to the community members themselves and will be accessed by vendors only on terms established by individual members. Nevertheless, members, assisted by the community organizer, will have significant incentive to provide selected vendors with access to this information. Vendors would then be able to access information on high-potential customers within the product category in general, not just on their own current customers. Virtual communities also generate information on demonstrated preferences, indicating that an attractive prospect may be on the verge of making another purchase (for example, a member of a travel community starts accessing information about Italy). Access to this kind of information, once again on terms defined by individual members, would enable vendors to target attractive prospects in a timely fashion.

- **Greater ability to tailor and add value to existing products and services:** Access to integrated transaction histories and the ability to interact with customers and potential customers improve the vendor's ability to understand individual buyer needs. By aggressively using this information to tailor products and to create product and service bundles, vendors can both expand the potential customer base and generate more revenue from each customer.

In addition to benefiting from elements specific to virtual communities, vendors will benefit from elements more broadly applicable to network environments. These include the following.

- **Lower capital investment in bricks and mortar:** Many vendors will not have to build costly branches or retail outlets to reach and sell to target customers in an on-line environment. For example, we estimate that a retail bank operating exclusively on the network could achieve a 30–40 percent cost advantage relative to a traditional retail bank operating branches.

- *Broader geographic reach:* Vendors will be able to reach much broader customer segments, freed from geographic constraints.

- *Disintermediation potential:* Given both the reduced need for investment in bricks and mortar and the enhanced ability to capture information about their end customers directly on-line, product manufacturers and service companies will be in a better position to deal directly with their end customers without the assistance of traditional intermediaries (retailers, wholesalers, distributors, or brokers).

Together, these add up to considerable opportunity for vendors. But virtual communities are not simply a stand-alone business opportunity that management can choose to address or ignore. By shifting power from the vendor to the customer, virtual communities will irreversibly alter the way large companies are managed.

Virtual communities are likely to change the way companies manage specific business functions, particularly those which operate at the customer interface, like marketing and sales. They offer the potential to reshape existing industry structures by redefining sources of advantage (for instance, by undermining the importance of scale). Virtual communities will present new ways for businesses to organize around core processes and broad practice or skill areas. And they'll accelerate the movement toward—and increase the effectiveness of—outsourcing and extended-enterprise networks.

THE CHALLENGE OF CHANGE

Bridging the profound gap between the way traditional businesses are run and the way virtual communities will be built and run represents the single greatest challenge for senior management of existing companies. Most will need to adopt a mental model very different from the one they have in place. They'll need to rethink their notions of where value can be created and how they can capture that value.

Coming to a new understanding of where value can be created will require perhaps the greatest cognitive leap for the organizer of the virtual community. This is because recognizing the new source of value creation means switching allegiance: those organizations most firmly aligned with their members, those that represent members' interests in dealing with vendors—not those which see their mission as helping vendors to sell more effectively to customers—will be in the best position to capture value. The business model thus shifts from one in which the organization "pushes" products or services on target customers toward one in which it acts as an agent for customers, representing and championing their interests as they seek improved access to resources. In this way, virtual communities create "reverse markets," where customers seek out vendors and deal with them on a much more level playing field in terms of information access. This shift in power has three key implications:

Most companies will need to do a complete rethink of what business they're in.

1. ***Members must be given the tools necessary to wield their new power:*** In particular, this means recognizing the power of member-to-member interaction and creating an environment in which member-generated content is encouraged and can be captured. This becomes the focal point of the community and its distinctive value. It means orchestrating the broadest possible range of high-quality, published content relevant to members. But it also means providing members with technology-based services (for example, search engines, agents, and bulletin boards) that will help them access other members with relevant insights and help them accumulate information quickly, easily, and cost effectively.

2. ***Members must be given ample opportunity to wield their new power:*** To wield power, members must have access to a broad range of competing and complementary vendors in a robust transaction environment where they can quickly and effectively compare products and services, execute transactions, and switch to other vendors if their expectations are not met.

3. ***Members must be given the chance to maximize the value they receive from information about themselves:*** Information about members is a powerful asset that will eventually be claimed by the members themselves. Those community organizers which are most helpful in facilitating members' capture of information and in maximizing its value to them will be the winners. This value includes monetary

value, but it also includes a range of services, especially searching, filtering, and analyzing information so as to enhance member learning. Rather than helping vendors target the customer, the primary focus of the community organizer will be to help customers identify appropriate vendors (or, more broadly, to help members find providers of what they need).

There are three more essential principles for senior managers to observe in planning and establishing the successful virtual community. The first will no doubt prove counterintuitive: member aggregation is more important than the type or amount of resources owned. Of course, some resources will be required to aggregate members, but senior management is often tempted to focus on resource ownership as the key metric for success. After all, these resources are clearly identifiable on a balance sheet. In contrast, members are not assets in an accounting sense, and in the early years they may not even be a source of revenue.

The second principle concerns planning for growth. Thoughtful selection of what will be the entry points into the community is crucial. As we will explain in chapters 3 and 5, virtual communities provide platforms for growth in a wide range of related businesses. Chapter 5 suggests that the specific nature and size of these growth options are likely to vary depending on the entry point selected by the community organizer—in other words, on the distinctive focus defining the community. These growth options will be hard to discern in advance, given high levels of uncertainty. And they will be even more difficult to value, given traditional "net present value" techniques.

The third principle again asks managers to develop a new mental model. It concerns the approach to organizing a business. In contrast to the traditional corporate enterprise, the virtual community will require flexible and organic approaches to organization. Seeding, feeding, and weeding represent much richer metaphors for on-line organizational design and evolution than detailed blueprints and plans. This organic approach to organization is driven in part by the need to be responsive to the emerging needs of community members and in part by the need to cultivate a new set of skills that will be most likely to emerge within the communities themselves. The leveraged entry strategies required to build virtual communities also demand the ability to manage a broad network of partners and providers, as well as the ability to create appropriate value-sharing mechanisms to motivate and focus these partners and providers. In general, the organic approach to organization will need to be shaped and balanced by a tight focus on the key economic levers driving value creation over time (such as member aggregation). Once again, the traditional culture of control typical to large corporations will be at odds with these new organizational forms.

This book is intended to drive action, first by persuading readers that virtual communities represent a powerful new vehicle for value creation, second by relating the general principles that will lead to success, and third by convincing readers that rewards will most likely accrue to those who move first and fast.

Failing to act may be the riskiest act of all. Not only will companies risk losing the opportunity represented by virtual communities, they will incur increasing risk that their core businesses will be exposed to attack by those who move more aggressively to build virtual communities. Virtual communities are already beginning to emerge; their continued growth will have widespread consequences for most traditional businesses. Those who ignore their potential power run the risk of being squeezed by new players in the game that understand both the stakes of winning and losing and the changing rules of the game.

2

reversing
markets

how customers gain

Early enthusiasts of on-line networks—
particularly the Internet—resisted the
idea that these networks might be used
for commercial purposes (as some still
do). But community and commerce need
not be at odds. Community in fact
provides a unique context in which
commerce can take place as customers
equip themselves with better information.
The result is a "reverse market" in which
power accrues to the customer. To become
profitable, the organizer of the virtual
community must understand and address
this newly empowered customer's needs.

I N THEIR RELATIONSHIPS WITH CUSTOMERS, vendors have long held the upper hand. This has to do with information. Access to information is a key determinant of bargaining power in any commercial transaction. If one party gains access to more information, that party tends to be able to extract more value from transactions than a party with access to less information.

In most markets today, vendors are armed with comparatively more information than their customers. They use this information to target the most attractive customers for their products or services and to engage in what economists call price discrimination—the practice of charging one customer one price and other customers another, depending on what the market will bear. Price discrimination is perfectly legal, to be sure, but it does illustrate one of the ways in which vendors tend to capture market surplus at their customers' expense.

Virtual communities are likely to turn these market dynamics upside down by creating "reverse markets"— markets in which the customer, armed with a growing amount of information, uses that information to search out vendors offering the best combination of quality and price tailored to his or her individual needs. In fact, the ability to access more information and thereby extract more value from vendors will ultimately be one of the major incentives drawing

Reverse markets mean vendors no longer have information on their side.

members into virtual communities. But members won't realize this benefit until their community reaches a certain size. It falls to the community organizer to address the interests and needs of members from the outset in order to establish a viable community.

THE NEED FOR VIRTUAL COMMUNITY

Virtual communities are not, ultimately, about aggregating information and other kinds of resources, although they certainly do that. Virtual communities are about aggregating people. People are drawn to virtual communities because they provide an engaging environment in which to connect with other people—sometimes only once, but more often in an ongoing series of interactions that create an atmosphere of trust and real insight. But what is the basis of this interaction? It is essentially based on people's desire to meet four basic needs: interest, relationship, fantasy, and transaction.

Virtual communities will differ significantly in terms of relative focus on these basic needs; some will emphasize one need more than the others. But few will be able to succeed if they address one need to the exclusion of the others. This is because the strength of virtual communities rests in their ability to address multiple needs simultaneously.

Interest

Most of us have some passionate interest. As consumers, many of us are enthusiastic about sports, entertainment, or vacation travel. Some have absorbing hobbies that range from collecting stamps to collecting recordings of folk music from different countries. Others are consumed by the never-ending challenge of beating the stock market. Many of us also have strong professional interests. We may want to develop a better understanding of broad industry trends, to learn about the latest techniques in improving salesforce productivity, or to make sure we have arrived at the best possible purchase decisions for components critical to our business.

Many early virtual communities targeted the interest need by aggregating a dispersed group of people who share interest and expertise in a specific topic. One of the most successful communities of interest emerging to date is Motley Fool, an electronic forum that two charismatic brothers, David and Tom Gardner, host on America Online. The

Gardners began Motley Fool for people interested in personal financial investment. They developed a portfolio of stock investments and invited people to comment on the choices made.

More broadly, a vast subculture has emerged around independent bulletin board services started and operated by individuals (rarely corporations) known as sysops (short for system operators) who are passionate about a specific topic. These bulletin boards have typically been accessed by dialing a telephone number unique to each board and connecting through a modem, but a growing number are now also accessible through the Internet. The groups of people drawn to these bulletin boards are remarkably diverse: from gun collectors to amateur astronomers seeking the latest information on a new comet. The ability to connect with others who share a narrow interest is a compelling draw for many people who otherwise might never have become computer literate.

Professionally focused bulletin boards are also successful. A number of industry and professional associations—for example, the American Bar Association, the American Medical Association, the Software Support Professionals Association, the Association for Information and Image Management—have created on-line services that enable members to share information on topics of common interest.

Relationship

At various stages in life, we encounter new, often intense, experiences that may draw us to others who've had a similar experience. Such traumatic events as the death of a loved one, divorce, or the diagnosis of a debilitating or fatal disease often bring fellow sufferers together. Many people develop addictions and need help to overcome them. More broadly, each stage in life presents its own challenges. Teenagers, new parents, and senior citizens have a need to share the experience of their particular time of life with peers. In the process, personal and often deep relationships may be formed.

Virtual communities give people with similar experiences the opportunity to come together—freed from the constraints of time and space—and form meaningful personal relationships. The Cancer Forum on CompuServe, for instance, provides support for cancer patients and their families. Participants talk about how they deal with the disease and exchange information on medical research, pain medication, test results, and protocols. And they can download literature on cancer from the forum's library. But the primary value of this sort of community seems to be based on its ability to bring people together to share personal experiences. Numerous other communities on the Internet are relationship focused. They include groups on divorce, widowhood, and infertility.

The members of a virtual community are its real creators.

One of the fastest growing such communities is SeniorNet, a virtual community of more than 18,000 members. SeniorNet is a nonprofit organization based in the United States seeking to build a community of computer-using seniors. Started as a research project at the University of San Francisco in 1986 by Dr. Mary Furlong, Senior-Net was incorporated in 1990. On her Web site, Furlong recounts her inspiration for SeniorNet: "My grandmother's life provided the model for SeniorNet. Here was a woman who had friends to whom she spoke every day. When I visited her, she would go across the street to the park, and people were there, sitting on park benches, and knew each other's names. It's that sense of community that I really felt was somehow lacking in our modern world."

SeniorNet now maintains forums targeted to senior citizens on America Online, Microsoft Network, and the Internet. The forums cover a broad terrain. There are, for instance, Christian Corner, Divorced Pals, Federal Retirees, and Senior Entrepreneur. The enthusiasm of members is captured by one senior citizen who participates in a SeniorNet gardening group and is developing an "electronic database of roses": "We are only beginning to imagine the people with whom we can collaborate." Furlong is clear about the role SeniorNet plays: "The most important aspect of SeniorNet is that the members are the producers. They are the creators. They are the talent. We're just stringing it together."

The success of SeniorNet is particularly surprising given the target demographic. Yet a 1994 survey cited by SeniorNet reveals that a rapidly growing number of senior citizens own computers. The promise of sharing common life experiences without having to leave home has driven many senior citizens to invest in their first computer and to sign up for training in the use of SeniorNet. In an effort to prepare more senior citizens to participate in the on-line world, SeniorNet helped start more than eighty SeniorNet Learning Centers around the United States.

Fantasy

Network environments also give people the opportunity to come together and explore new worlds of fantasy and entertainment. A unique characteristic of these environments is the freedom they give participants to "try out" new personas and to engage in role-playing games where everything seems possible.

One of the earliest and darkest forms of community to emerge on networks were MUDs (reflecting an early interest in role playing fashioned after the game Dungeons and Dragons, MUD initially stood for Multi-User Dungeons; it now represents the more sophisticated Multi-User Dimensions). MUDs are organized environments where players can assume a broad range of fantasy roles and interact with each other in elaborate and evolving games that may stretch over years. These can became such consuming experiences that college health administrators began to express concern about "MUD addiction," as college students sacrificed study time to spend hours every day in their favorite MUD environment. A complex collective of role-playing game environments has blossomed on the network, known by such variants as MOO, MUSH, MUCK, MUSE, and MUX.

To give an example, in one MUD on America Online a participant can pretend to be a medieval baron at the Red Dragon Inn. In this fantasy area, visitors exercise their imagination and participate (through typed, electronic chat) in the creation of an ongoing story about life at the inn. Over a two-month cycle, players can accumulate enough wins to advance through a complex hierarchy of titles, including apprentice, sorcerer, magician, and wizard.

Not all fantasy games are so removed from daily life, however. In the Internet-based sports community ESPNet, for instance, participants can create their own sports teams (using the names of real players), which then compete against teams created by other participants. Winners are determined by incorporating assessments of the performance of the real players during the season.

It's not hard to imagine the application of fantasy to detailed simulation games in business-to-business virtual communities that would help members internalize key business principles and observe their impact in interactions with others. Can it be long before marketers compete in "Widgetland" for the largest market share by applying the latest techniques of Continuous Relationship Marketing? Or before lawyers litigate mock cases in virtual court to see how certain strategies play out in front of a judge and jury?

Transaction

The need to "transact," broadly defined, is being met on-line through the trading of information between participants. In fact, the notion of barter, or fair exchange, has been an important element of the culture and etiquette of the early Internet. But it will take some time for the virtual community to address the transaction need in the full economic sense of the word. Its ability to do so is likely to be limited by both technology constraints (continuing concerns about security and authentication on the Internet, for example) and the relatively small number of members and vendors now aggregated in any one space. Nevertheless, addressing this fourth need is a natural extension of initiatives in which members with a strong interest in certain kinds of products and services are gathering to exchange information and experiences regarding purchases.

For example, Motley Fool has already begun to sell books and other products related to financial investment. Can it be long before Motley Fool presents members with the opportunity to interact directly with on-line brokers to execute their stock trades? Already, many independent bulletin board services targeted to collectors offer "classified ad" spaces where collectors can buy and sell items in their collections.

Alternatively, some initiatives designed specifically for the purpose of sales transactions are likely to evolve into more fully developed virtual communities. Virtual Vineyards, a Web-based service that sells wines, addresses a very specific transaction need. The Virtual Vineyard site offers visitors information on wines, and lists special deals on attractively priced offerings. Most of the wines listed are from small vineyards and are usually difficult to obtain in the average liquor store. Visitors can purchase the wines directly from Virtual Vineyards, using an on-line form, or they can call the on-line service. Although visitors can post e-mail to the organizer of the site (as well as questions to the Cork Dork), they cannot yet trade information with each other. Adding that capability might add value for the site's visitors, making it a true community.

In a business-to-business context, Nets, Inc., is an example of an emerging market space that aggregates buyers and sellers of certain kinds of engineering products. Nets brings together more than 200,000 buyers and 4,500 sellers of industrial products. Major categories of products covered by the Nets service include measurement and sensor equipment, control systems, and manufacturing and engineering software.

Nets, Inc., helps to facilitate commercial transactions with a broad range of services, including a Catalog Library where buyers can search through detailed product catalogs from manufacturers and distributors, a Hot New Products service providing information on new products, and a Surplus Equipment Service that helps members locate discontinued, hard-to-find, or previously owned products at discounted prices. Other services of interest to members include an Online Career Fair, which posts listings of jobs and of seminars on specific products or technologies.

A powerful brew

Because the virtual community's ability to address not just one of these needs but all of them is so valuable—and because this ability distinguishes the community from other forms of on-line activity, such as electronic malls and newspapers—it will be useful to look at a couple of examples of how it works. We have already cited ESPNet as an emerging virtual community that addresses the many needs of its members. It clearly plays to the interest need by providing a rich mix of information and interaction on specific sports. Forming and "playing" virtual sports teams against other members addresses a strong fantasy need. ESPNet sells sports memorabilia in its "ZoneStore," thereby addressing a transaction need. The site also promotes an ESPN MasterCard credit card that can be ordered on-line. By providing a rich set of communication forums for its members, ESPNet is also increasing the opportunity for personal relationships to develop among those who share a passion for sports.

In a business-to-business context, virtual communities can also address a broad range of needs. One can imagine a virtual community targeted to owners of a small business in which they would be able to exchange information on issues specific to their needs (how to set up a payroll system or comply with certain regulatory requirements, for instance). The virtual community might also offer simulation games that let the small-business owner learn and test certain financing techniques. It might offer not only information on the best photocopiers for a small-business operation but also the means through which to buy one on-line. Special bulletin boards and chat areas might be established for sharing experiences at different stages of small-business development (start-up, going public) or for sharing the personal challenges of small-business ownership (maintaining the right balance between business and personal life, when and how to involve relatives in the business).

A POWER SHIFT

We have so far suggested that some of the initial power of virtual communities involves their ability to aggregate people in environments that address some combination of four basic needs they experience in their professional and personal lives. The real commercial potential of virtual communities, however, will begin to emerge only as they aggregate a critical mass of members and develop rich transaction capabilities. Such on-line forums as Nets, Inc., and Agriculture Online (targeting farmers) have announced their intention to add transaction capabilities to services that began as information and communication sites. Virtual communities have the potential to drive a major shift in power from vendor to customer and, in the process, to shift the capture of surplus economic value from vendors to customers.

Figure 2-1A presents a classic microeconomics supply and demand curve, with the straight horizontal line at the intersection of supply and demand representing the market price in a standard customer-vendor relationship. Figure 2-1B illustrates the impact of virtual communities in shifting surplus value from vendors to customers. Note that the market price now tracks the supply curve more closely, reflecting the increasingly auctionlike environments likely to prevail in virtual communities as reverse markets take hold. At that point, when customers want to make a purchase, they notify appropriate vendors and solicit bids. The bidding process tends to create a "minimarket" out of each transaction opportunity, where the clearing price is the winning bid, typically offered by the vendor best able to tailor price and function to the needs of the customer.

The key elements driving this shift in power—aggregation of

Figure 2-1A Surplus Shifts from Vendor . . .

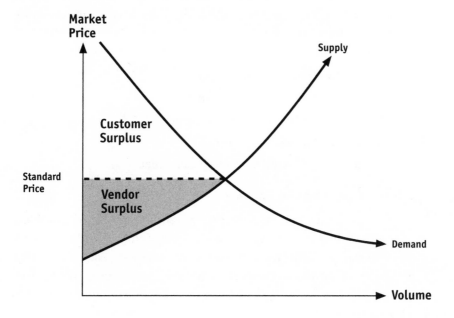

Figure 2-1B . . . to Customer in the Virtual Community Environment

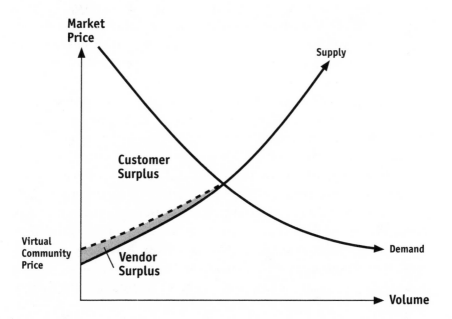

purchasing power, improved access to information by customers, vendor choice, and the presence of a highly motivated intermediary who is rewarded for helping to put into place the first three elements—provide the basis for a more systematic exploration of the five characteristics that define the virtual community, introduced in chapter 1:

1. Distinctive focus as to membership.
2. Integration of content and communication.
3. Emphasis on member-generated content.
4. Choice among competing vendors.
5. Commercially motivated community organizers.

Aggregation of purchasing power

Virtual communities help to aggregate purchasing power by providing a compelling environment that draws in new members and by providing a rich array of means for members to connect with each other. This aggregation of purchasing power is helped enormously by the first defining characteristic of a virtual community: a distinctive focus as to membership.

First defining characteristic: Distinctive focus as to membership. Virtual communities differ from broader network environments like the Internet or traditional on-line services such as America Online or CompuServe in that they target a specific type of member. Having a distinctive focus is vital to members from the outset. They need to know where they can go to find others who share their interests and needs as well as to find resources such as published content and vendors that have been conveniently aggregated to serve their particular needs. The virtual community should be a repository for member-generated content that is relevant to members' distinctive interests. It should take the vast, untamed wilderness of the network and harness its power to serve the needs of users.

By providing a distinctive focus, virtual communities also accelerate the process of aggregating purchasing power. Almost any conceivable community would have a distinctive set of transaction interests and needs. A personal finance community gathers together individuals who are active investors in stocks and mutual funds. A virtual community for lawyers brings together individuals and firms with a strong interest in accessing legal information services and certain kinds of expertise (forensic medicine, private investigators for criminal defense attorneys, and so on).

These individuals often represent the most attractive purchasers of specific categories of products and services. For example, market research suggests that readers of travel magazines spend on average three times more on travel than the average consumer. It is reasonable to expect that, especially in the early years, members of travel-oriented virtual communities will display a similar skew in spending within the travel category.

Through their distinctive focus, virtual communities thus serve as magnets, conjoining customers who share common purchase profiles and who collectively represent a disproportionate amount of the purchase activity in specific transaction categories. In isolation, this defining characteristic of a virtual community would be interesting in the same way that specialty magazines provide a similar aggregation of audiences for advertisers to reach. But in combination with the other defining characteristics of a virtual community, outlined below, this aggregation of purchasing power becomes the first step in driving a fundamental shift in purchasing power. There is potential power in numbers, and virtual communities will bring purchasers together in environments that will make them far more effective in leveraging their collective power.

Improved access to information

Virtual communities not only gather potential purchasers together, but they also arm them with far more information than they have typically been able to access conveniently and cost effectively in the past. As we said earlier in this chapter, moving away from this traditional information asymmetry is likely to create reverse markets in which power shifts to the customer. These reverse markets highlight two other defining characteristics of virtual communities—integration of content and communication, and emphasis on member-generated content.

Second defining characteristic: Integration of content and communication. Networks like America Online and the Internet differ from conventional networks and traditional media in their ability to integrate content and communication. Traditional media tend to be one-way broadcast vehicles—examples are magazines, books, records, TV programs, movies—delivering content to a target audience. With few exceptions (notably, letters to the editor, talk radio, and television talk shows), these media offer little opportunity for the audience to interact with the publishers, much less with each other. In contrast, conventional networks like the telephone network offer rich opportunities for communication but relatively limited ability to capture, store, and retrieve content.

Virtual communities harness the unique capabilities of these new networks by providing environments in which communication and content are not only available but also tightly integrated. Thus, individuals coming together in a chat room can retrieve and "pull in" content relevant to their discussion. Participants in a bulletin board can access prior postings and then post questions to one or more of the authors of the prior postings. Moderators on bulletin boards can post a recent news item or quote from a book to spur a new round of discussion between participants. Authors of published content can be queried for clarification or more specific information much more easily than they can in traditional print.

This kind of integration of communication and content can be illustrated in the example of a hypothetical travel community. Such a community might bring together a broad array of published content, ranging from conventional travel guides to travel magazines and specialized newsletters, as well as on-line brochures and information from tourist bureaus and specific vendor information (airline schedules, hotel information, and so forth). At the same time, the community would provide a rich set of forums for communication between travelers, including bulletin boards on which travelers can post questions to one another (parents inquiring about child friendly resorts, seniors looking for travel companions) and special hosted events where renowned (and not so renowned) experts would be available for questioning.

A key role of the community organizer is to aggregate appropriate published content for members. In large part, this means serving as an agent, searching out and gathering relevant content while filtering out unreliable or low-quality content. The community organizer must commit to meeting a certain quality standard. Anyone who has "surfed the Net" and waded through incredible masses of "shovel ware" (material published first in old media that is then "shoveled" into new media with no attempt to make use of the properties of those new media) and vendor press releases in a vain attempt to get the answer to a specific question from a reliable source can appreciate the added value of the community organizer in prescreening and organizing information.

Since information in virtual communities can come from other members rather than published "experts," the community organizer also plays a valuable role in "certifying" the authenticity and qualifications of other members providing such information. Members who routinely provide false, or self-serving, information might be exiled from the community or, at minimum, muzzled.

The merging of content and communication in a community environment makes available a rich information resource to members who are contemplating a specific kind of purchase. In a travel community, a member contemplating a trip to Florence might quickly scan ten different published guides to hotels in the city, review member-generated ratings of the hotels, and then post a question to a bulletin board asking for tips from members who have been to Florence in the past couple of months. The relative value of these suggestions might be evaluated by consulting profiles of the members to determine if they have similar interests and experience. If the member is confused by contradictory or incomplete information obtained from these services, he or she might contact individual authors or members to seek clarification. As these communities evolve, the range, richness, reliability, and timeliness of the information available to members as they consider purchases is likely to be far greater than that of any information available through more conventional means, thereby increasing the likelihood of purchase.

Third defining characteristic: Emphasis on member-generated content.

A key assumption driving the formation of virtual communities is that members will over time derive greater value from member-generated content than from more conventional forms of "published" content. Member-generated content is typically produced in real time in chat areas and accumulated in the postings to bulletin boards.

Some people remain skeptical that member-generated content will have greater value than content published by well-known "experts" in their relevant fields. Michael Kinsley, former editor of the *New Republic* and now managing editor of Microsoft's on-line publishing venture *Slate,* was widely quoted for his observation at an industry conference that the guests at a restaurant would much rather have their meal prepared by a trained chef than by the person who happened to be sitting at the table next to them.

Such observations, while entertaining, overlook a fundamental point, which is that virtual communities will aggregate an enormous collective expertise that could not possibly be matched by any individual expert, no matter how well trained or experienced. In many cases, the value may not be so much in the experience and knowledge of any one individual but in the comparative experiences and perspectives of many individuals. A good example of this concept are the Zagat's guides that have become a staple for restaurant-goers across the United States. The value of these guides is not that they present the perspective of one expert

What good is one "expert's" opinion in the face of enormous collective expertise?

but that they provide us with a broad cross-section of perspectives and experiences of people who share a passion for food.

It is precisely this kind of expertise and experience that virtual communities do such a good job of marshaling. No combination of "published" experts could match the collective insight and experience of a community of people who share a passionate interest.

Amazon.com, a rapidly growing gathering spot for book lovers on the Internet, illustrates this focus on member-generated content. While featuring book reviews by reviewers from the *New York Times*, Amazon.com has also established "Amazon.com Community," where members are not only allowed but encouraged to post their own reviews. In fact, Amazon.com offers members a prize of up to $1,000 worth of books in a Book Recommendation Contest. Such devices not only aggregate a large amount of information on books for the benefit of all members, but they also encourage a feeling of greater involvement in the community and help to stimulate the sale of more books in the process.

In this way, virtual communities dramatically augment the information and expertise available to their members as they make purchase decisions. The sharing of information *between* customers in given transaction categories has until now been a relatively haphazard and unreliable event. It is this capability that takes the aggregated purchasing power in a virtual community and transforms it into collective behavior that can rapidly and decisively determine vendor success and failure.

Of all the features of a virtual community, this is the one that makes vendors most uncomfortable. A forum in which customers talk among themselves on a continuing basis is threatening. If customers are pleased with a product or service, word of mouth (or word of keyboard) spreads rapidly and vendors benefit. But the reverse is also true. Vendors who offer substandard products or services find themselves quickly and effectively exposed.

Vendor choice

Virtual communities do more than aggregate members; they also aggregate vendors offering products or services likely to be of interest to members. By providing an environment in which members can interact with individual vendors as well as purchase their products or services, virtual communities set into motion a dynamic that drives the shift in power from vendor to customer. Unlike traditional retail environments, where customers are presented with a limited number of vendors—"take them or leave them"—virtual communities make it possible for customers to search actively for a broader range of vendors and offerings (shelf space is not a major constraint in virtual space) and, where appropriate, to enter into transaction-specific negotiations with vendors.

Fourth defining characteristic: Choice of competing vendor offers. Virtual communities might start by offering only one vendor's products or services. This might be especially true for virtual communities organized or sponsored by a single vendor. However, we speculate that few virtual communities, if any, will be able to sustain themselves in this manner.

Put yourself in the place of a potential community member interested in audio-video equipment. Would you consider joining an audio-video community sponsored by a vendor of audio-video equipment that limits the availability of information and product selection to its products alone? Or would you want to join a competing community that aggregates information and product offers from an array of competing vendors and that gives you the opportunity to interact with audiophiles and videophiles who debate the performance of these competing vendors?

In any virtual community with a reasonably significant transaction opportunity related to the distinctive focus of the community, the opportunity to select from competing vendors is likely to drive member affiliation over time. It is precisely this opportunity to select among competing vendors that will make it possible for customers to extract greater value from vendors. And, as mentioned previously, this is also what makes it possible for virtual communities to build reverse markets.

Amazon.com, cited above, provides some early examples of the reverse market in action. Amazon.com's directories allow members to search through and purchase from more than 1 million titles of books in print. These searches can be made by keyword as well as the more conventional author, title, and subject headings. An Editors' Notification Service also alerts members to new titles appearing in prespecified subject categories. Book buyers from Bahrain, Bosnia, and Guam have more book titles available to them, and more information about the books available, than anyone visiting the largest bookstore in New York or Frankfurt.

This turns the traditional market model, in which vendors seek out customers, on its head. Virtual communities put customers in this more powerful position by providing them with a rich source of vendor information, forums in which to interact with other customers who have dealt with specific vendors, and the capability of interacting with specific vendors to negotiate the most advantageous terms of sale. In many cases, virtual communities are likely to offer auction spaces where customers can post their needs and create bidding wars between competing vendors to obtain the best price. Technology enabling the community organizer to act as an agent for members, quickly and efficiently searching out the best offer available, will have a huge role to play. Amazon.com offers Eyes, an automated search agent, that automatically sends a member an e-mail when a certain book comes out in paperback or a favorite author publishes a new book. Increasingly, customers will pit one vendor against another to secure the best deal for themselves.

Motivated intermediaries

Putting all these elements into place to make a successful virtual community is a far from trivial task. In some cases, this effort will be undertaken by individuals who have a passion for a particular topic area, carrying on the voluntarist, uncommercial tradition of the early Internet. We believe, however, that this task will be increasingly undertaken by individuals and corporations who see the power in this new business model and are motivated by the opportunity to turn a profit.

Fifth defining characteristic: Commercially motivated community organizers. We acknowledge and salute the early pioneers of the network who in organizing virtual communities were not driven by commercial motives and who, in many cases, were driven by anticommercial values. Many valuable lessons have been learned from their efforts. Many uncommercial virtual communities will continue to emerge and play a valuable role on networks. Bringing about the shift in power from vendor to customer, however, will fall to the commercially motivated community organizer. Aggregating a critical mass of purchasing power in virtual communities will require significant resources and a reasonably long time horizon. In many cases, these resources are unlikely to be available unless an attractive return can be earned. In other cases, the resources may be available, but the prospect of an attractive return will help to accelerate their deployment. Furthermore, competition between community organizers for attractive returns will encourage innovation, helping the entire concept and workings of the virtual community to develop and mature more quickly.

As we will show in chapter 3, the economics of virtual communities can be very attractive from the perspective of the community organizer. Powerful profit incentives will therefore drive the formation and growth of virtual communities on the network. Since much of this profit hinges on recognizing and exploiting the opportunity to shift power from vendors to customers, community organizers will have a strong motivation to overcome potential vendor resistance and invest the necessary resources. Community organizers who champion their members' cause in dealing with vendors will be richly rewarded; those who continue to approach transactions from the perspective of the vendor are likely to find profitability elusive. Market mechanisms will therefore help to accelerate the profound shift in power promised by virtual communities.

THE POWER OF PREDOMINANCE

As virtual communities evolve on the network, their value to members will expand. As we have discussed, the early value of communities will rest largely on their capacity to address the passions of their members. As a critical mass of members and purchasing power aggregate within a community, it will give members the opportunity to extract still greater value from the vendors they do business with. In even later stages, virtual communities are likely to offer value to a broader range of people. These more casual buyers will participate in communities largely for the sake of purchasing products and services rather than pursuing an avid interest. Exploring the virtual community will become for them an alternative to visiting the shopping mall or contacting the local distributor. At this point, the value of virtual communities will become their predominance. Because of the volume of transactions they generate, they will become the preferred place to shop for large segments of customers.

THE VENDOR'S DILEMMA . . .

At this point readers might fairly ask, If virtual communities are going to shift power from vendor to customer, why would a vendor choose to participate in (as distinct from organize) such a community? Why not simply boycott these new business environments and deprive customers of the chance to exercise their power? As vendors begin to realize the potential implications of participation in virtual communities, this kind of reaction is certain to be expressed by senior management.

Of course, if virtual communities are unable to aggregate a critical mass of members, vendors have little to worry about. They can stand on the sidelines and wait for this latest fad to pass. On the other hand, if virtual communities prove to be sufficiently powerful to aggregate a critical mass of members, vendors face a difficult dilemma. Take Motley Fool. Once it accumulates millions of active financial investors, wouldn't it offer mutual funds and other vendors of financial services a very attractive audience?

If all vendors were to resist participating in virtual communities, they might prevent virtual communities from advancing to the next stage and helping members extract more value from vendors. But all vendors are not alike. The smaller vendor and the new entrant to the market in particular stand to benefit from participation in virtual communities. Because they typically have relatively limited existing business, the prospect of the potential margin squeeze resulting from a shift in power from vendor to customer is much less threatening than it is for vendors with well-established market positions.

Figure 2-2 highlights the good news for vendors. The combined effects of lowering transaction costs for both vendors and customers should shift both the supply (1) and demand (2) curves to the right. As a result, the supply and demand curves intersect farther to the right than in the days before virtual communities, suggesting that aggregate transaction activity will increase (3). How much transaction activity will increase and what will be the net effect once the shift in surplus from vendors to customers is considered will vary significantly from market to market.

If any smaller vendor or new entrant breaks ranks and chooses to play in the virtual community environment, larger vendors face substantial risk. Should they hold back and hope that virtual communities prove to be a marginal environment for transactions, at least for their product or service category? If they do hold back and virtual communities become significant transaction environments, they risk losing market share to those vendors who do participate. Once lost, that market share may prove difficult to regain. As members' loyalty to their community and its members increases, they will become less and less likely

Figure 2-2 Market Expansion in the Virtual Community

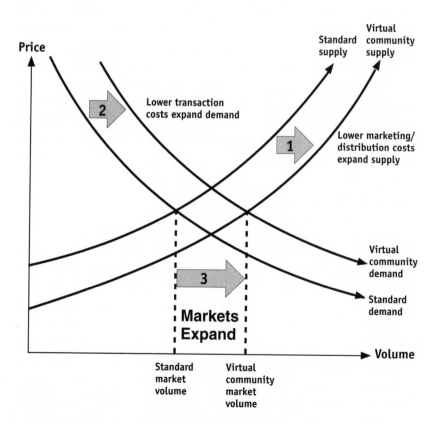

to switch to another community. On the other hand, if these large vendors choose to participate, their participation will further increase the attractiveness of the virtual community as a transaction environment and will therefore increase the risk of a shift in power.

Given the attractiveness of the membership of many of the virtual communities emerging on the network and the likely value to members of executing transactions within the virtual community, it is likely that small vendors and new entrants will be aggressive in exploiting the opportunity to expand their markets.

Smaller vendors will be the first to break ranks.

If they are, it will probably be only a matter of time before large vendors find it necessary to join as well.

Although it is still too early in the development of virtual communities to offer many examples of this dynamic at work, ParentsPlace, a site dedicated to meeting the needs of parents, represents one illustration of early transaction activity. ParentsPlace offers certain products for sale, including baby foods and shampoos. The vendors are small players: Earth's Best Baby Foods and Mustela (respectively). Larger vendors have yet to decide whether to participate, but if the community grows to a critical mass of members and transaction activity grows, can they afford not to join? ParentsPlace has already started to attract smaller retail intermediaries like Delivered with Love, The Breastfeeding Shop, and Natural Baby Company, which are collectively making available a broad range of products targeted to the parents of small children. Once again, though, the larger retailers have yet to participate in ParentsPlace.

. . . AND THE OPPORTUNITY

It is not long since the term *virtual community*—at least in a commercial context—was considered new and innovative. All too soon, even casual observers must have lost count of the number of initiatives that called themselves communities springing up on the Internet and other network environments. It now seems that any Web site can lay claim to the mantle of community, even if all the site offers is a few pages of text and graphics.

If we apply the five defining characteristics of virtual community outlined earlier, this abundance of so-called communities dissolves. In fact, we cannot yet point to a single example of a virtual community that robustly incorporates all five of the defining characteristics. To fulfill their powerful potential, virtual communities must ultimately exhibit all five of these defining characteristics. Anything less will diminish the communities' potential impact.

If the virtual community as we have described it would be such a powerful enterprise, why can't we find more examples of communities in full bloom? The answer may be that, like many other business ventures with power and potential, they are not that easy to pull off. In fact, the notion of the virtual community represents a fundamental shift in mindset, especially for senior managers of well-established companies who have grown up in a very different world, driven by a very different set of assumptions about what leads to business success. Understood in this light, it is not at all surprising that at this early stage we can't find more examples of well-developed virtual communities. In fact, it is remarkable that there are so many examples of experimentation with elements of the virtual community model.

To illustrate clearly the required shift in mindset, it is useful to contrast a traditional publisher's or vendor's mental model of business value with that which should be held by the virtual community organizer. A traditional publisher or vendor is likely to believe that on-line customers would find the greatest value in being able to access individual resources—say, an on-line magazine, a retail bank, or an audio equipment vendor. The extent to which this businessperson would admit the value of interactivity would be to acknowledge that value in dealings between member and author/publisher or member and product/service vendor. Finally, the publisher or vendor would conclude that while marginal value *might* be accrued by aggregating resources on the network, the bulk of it would be captured by the individual publisher or vendor rather than the aggregator of the resources.

In contrast, the virtual community organizer would argue that the distinctive value of on-line environments is their ability to capture and accumulate member-generated content (for example, member reviews of vendor offerings, member "tips," member experiences). If this is true, it follows that the real focus of interactivity is interactivity between the community members themselves, and that interactivity with vendors and publishers serves only to enhance the value of interaction among members. This perspective leads to the view that value over time will concentrate in "shared" community spaces (bulletin boards, chat areas, and the like) and that this value will be largely captured by the members themselves and the organizers of these shared community spaces.

The differences in these mental models become clear when we look at the series of pragmatic choices that managers will have to make as they consider bringing business activity on-line. For example, would a vendor create a space where its customers could congregate freely and exchange information and perspectives about the vendor's products? Most vendors today would say no. At an even further extreme, would a vendor or publisher create a space where members could access not only the vendor's or publisher's own products but also those of its competitors? Such an approach would be viewed as heresy in most boardrooms today.

When we look out on the network today, we see a staggering array of business initiatives, some of which contain elements of the virtual community model we have been describing and many of which bear little resemblance to it. Major on-line services like America Online and CompuServe do not qualify as virtual communities as we have defined them here; they are not distinguished by a distinctive focus in terms of the members or content they are seeking to aggregate. Instead, they seek to acquire a broad mix of subscribers, representing a disparate collection of interests, and intend to provide these subscribers with a network environment that will serve most of their on-line needs.

Still, if we look closely at these on-line services, we do see some signs of emerging virtual communities. America Online in particular seems to have seized on the notion of community in a powerful way and offers examples of emerging communities in its Motley Fool and Red Dragon Inn. In fact, AOL's success in expanding its subscriber base at a much faster pace than CompuServe or Prodigy has less to do with its marketing efforts than with the way it caught on to the importance of user interaction and communication. America Online grew its subscriber base by almost 3.6 million members in the two years from 1993 to 1995, while CompuServe grew by 1.9 million members and Prodigy grew barely at all, adding fewer than 200,000 new members (net). Prodigy was slow to adjust its business model from a content "broadcast" model to a community model. As a result, it has been left behind, struggling to develop an architecture more suited to user communication than access to on-line newspapers.

On-line information services such as Lexis-Nexis are not virtual communities either—or at least not yet. Although Lexis offers a rich menu of content and has the defining characteristic of serving the legal community, it does not blend into its content the communication capabilities that would allow users to interact. At present, it is an on-line service focused on meeting the information needs of lawyers. It is not a community.

Another form of on-line site is the virtual shopping mall, an example being marketplace MCI. Like the information services, these malls do not encourage participant communication. And, like AOL, they do not have a single defining characteristic. Consequently, they face quite a challenge—offering customers a better range of products, or better prices, or an easier transaction than they might get by traveling to a store, picking up a catalog, or dialing an 800 number. Perhaps this is why MCI recently announced that it would be closing down marketplace MCI.

Similarly, many corporate sites on the World Wide Web fail to stimulate interaction between visitors. Certainly these Web sites offer more to the user than a magazine advertisement in terms of graphics and product information, but is this all that customers want?

Many media companies are putting their content on the Internet or on on-line services. Companies such as Time-Warner have made a considerable investment in putting some of their major publications on-line. But many on-line publications remain just that—traditional publications that take little advantage of what the virtual community has to offer. On-line interaction is often limited to a "letters to the editor" forum. These publishers seem reluctant to give up control of the medium to their "readers," for surely that control traditionally belongs to the journalist. That may be the case in print, but on-line publication is different. The journalist is no longer in control in the on-line world, or at least not obviously so. Instead, the journalist becomes a catalyst for interactions between members of the community.

In the course of this book we will show how virtual communities may bring change to a number of traditional roles in surprising ways. But it is precisely because these changes are surprising, and because they could be so profound, that our sympathy is with those corporate experimenters who are still in the process of understanding—and adapting to—the challenges and opportunities of this new medium.

Individual users are also experimenting with changes in behavior as they come on-line. The evidence of what is already happening on-line suggests that individuals and businesses have a considerably more practical yet ambitious view of what this new arena can offer them. For example, more than 100,000 doctors get medical news and prescription information on-line, and doctors are beginning to trade diagnostic case examples in discussion forums, one being Physicians Online. Representatives of the garment industry gather in the Virtual Garment Center to exchange information and explore transaction opportunities. Vendors and contractors in the paint and coatings industry exchange product and application information on the Paint/Coatings Net.

While no one organization has yet fulfilled the potential of the successful virtual community, the good news is that there is a business model in place and that some organizations have launched promising initiatives in the direction of that model. For the aggressive vendor, this situation represents an exceptional opportunity to launch one or more virtual community initiatives. The next chapter outlines the economics and the potential for value creation involved in doing so.

3

the new economics of virtual communities

The virtual community is not only a vehicle for shifting power from vendor to customer. For the community organizer, it's also a powerful vehicle for creating wealth. But traditional economic analysis won't account for its huge potential for growth; it doesn't recognize the size of the opportunity or the key contributors of value. What fuels the value creation that takes place in a virtual community is the economics of increasing returns.

IT DOESN'T COST MUCH—YET—TO GET STARTED
in the virtual community business. Virtual communities require relatively limited capital investment up front, and much of this investment is in fact not in technology but in member acquisition and support. Those who expect an immediate return on this investment, however, may be frustrated by substantial near-term pressures on profitability. These pressures are likely to make the near-term economics of virtual communities uncertain and challenging for the community organizer.

In this chapter we examine the economics of organizing a virtual community. We spell out where the revenues come from and where the costs are to be incurred. And we look at how increasing returns can be harnessed to accelerate and magnify revenue growth and return on investment.

THE ECONOMICS OF INCREASING RETURNS

The potential for virtual communities to create wealth is heavily shaped by the cumulative and reinforcing effects of increasing returns. A good understanding of the dynamics of increasing returns is therefore essential for community organizers. In particular, organizers will need to understand the revenue growth pattern that is distinctive of certain types of increasing returns businesses. This pattern involves a gradual buildup of revenues followed by a sharp acceleration coupled with a steady decline in unit costs as time passes.

Corporations such as Microsoft and Federal Express—businesses that eventually generated billions in dollars of revenues—took many years to reach significant scale. (See figure 3-1, which shows the classic pattern of growth fueled by increasing returns in four business areas.) For community organizers, significant revenues are unlikely to be forthcoming until certain thresholds, or "gates," have been passed. This means that initial invest-

ments are likely to be made in an environment of uncertainty and risk. This uncertainty is mitigated somewhat by the fact that organizers won't need to make excessive financial commitment up front to set increasing returns dynamics into motion—provided, that is, that they get in the game early. The costs of joining later quickly become prohibitive.

Even Microsoft and Federal Express found it slow going early on.

Increasing returns can take a number of forms. In their simplest form, increasing returns accrue when a business incurs large up-front expenditures to develop a new product or service and the incremental cost of producing each incremental unit of the product or service is minimal. This is often the case in the software business, where the cost of developing software can be quite significant and where manufacturing costs are negligible.

Another common form of increasing returns involves the learning

Figure 3-1 Growth of Increasing Returns Businesses

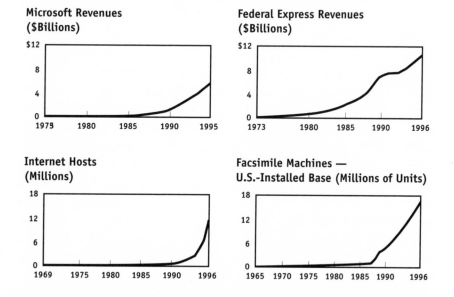

Microsoft Revenues ($Billions)

Federal Express Revenues ($Billions)

Internet Hosts (Millions)

Facsimile Machines — U.S.-Installed Base (Millions of Units)

curve, or experience curve, effects that most businesses realize over time. With each doubling in units sold, businesses typically achieve a certain percentage reduction in the cost of making and delivering that product or service to the customer. (Often there are also substantial learning effects in terms of skill building.) Therefore, the more you make, the more you benefit in terms of lower unit costs.

A third kind of increasing returns leverages network effects: the more units of product or service that are deployed, the more valuable each unit becomes. A simple example of this form of increasing returns is provided by the early history of the fax machine, a penetration-dependent product. An installed base of one fax machine is useless—to whom will its owner send faxes? But as each new fax machine is sold and deployed, the value of every other fax machine increases because there are more opportunities for communication. Think also of Federal Express. The more distribution nodes in the Federal Express network, the more valuable the overall service becomes.

Unlike the first two forms of increasing returns, which tend to display a uniform exponential revenue or cost curve, this third form of increasing returns is often characterized by one or more inflection points—revenue will slowly ramp up until the inflection point is reached, and then revenue growth accelerates. Take the fax example. There is likely to be some minimal penetration threshold below which a fax machine has practically no value, but once the penetration threshold is reached, the demand for additional fax machines really takes off. This pattern is evident in each of the four graphs in figure 3-1.

Virtual communities display all three forms of increasing returns dynamics. First, initial investment is required not only to "build" the virtual community environment (design the user interface, develop and deploy initial community services and offerings, develop and install data capture capability—more details below) but also to reach a critical mass of members. Second, significant learning effects are likely to be realized given the relatively early stage of business development (a doubling of unit volume is more quickly achieved than for more mature businesses, where a doubling of unit volume can take a long time to achieve). Finally, substantial network effects accrue in virtual community initiatives given the value of interaction between members. The community that has few members to interact will have little value relative to a community with many members. Moreover, few members will attract few, if any, published content providers, advertisers, or vendors, further reducing the value of the community to both its members and the organizer. For all these reasons, virtual communities are likely to follow the increasing returns model.

SOURCES OF REVENUE FOR THE VIRTUAL COMMUNITY

Getting a handle on the increasing returns model means understanding the ways in which the varying forms of increasing returns play out in the virtual community setting. To help build this understanding, we'll first spend some time describing the sources of revenue in a virtual community. Then we'll be ready to describe the self-reinforcing dynamic loops that shape the growth of revenue streams over time.

Virtual communities can tap into a number of potential fee-based revenue streams of the type that characterize on-line sites today, as outlined in the following table:

Type of Revenues	Description
Subscription fees	A fixed monthly charge for participation in the community
Usage fees	A charge based on the number of hours of usage or the number of "pages" accessed or some combination of the two
Member fees	
Content delivery fees	A charge for downloading specific information, such as a company investment report or a magazine article
Service fees	A charge for specialized services, such as a notification service when specified vendor products are offered for sale at predetermined prices

In addition, as the virtual community builds its membership, advertising and transaction commission revenues become more viable sources of revenue. Unlike subscription or usage fees, which are likely to vary directly with member growth, advertising and transaction revenues typically require a critical mass of audience or customers; advertisers and vendors won't be interested in participating in any virtual community in a meaningful way until this mass is reached. The critical mass necessary to trigger these revenue streams will vary with the market focus of the advertisers and vendors relevant to the community and the "reach" and pricing of competing media or channels.

Early forms of on-line advertising revenue stem from "banner" or icon-type ads inserted in one or more of the "pages" of a site. Over time, this advertising revenue is likely to include more targeted forms of advertising, such as banners or e-mail messages customized for individual users. Pricing of this advertising is also likely to evolve. Currently, advertising is largely priced using traditional media CPM ($ cost per thousand hits, *hits* being the number of viewers of an ad), although there is a move under way led by such advertisers as Procter & Gamble to shift to a cost per "click through" approach, where the advertiser pays based on the number of viewers of the ad who "click through" to get more information from the advertiser.

These pricing models are likely to evolve even further, reflecting the tight linkage in on-line environments between an advertisement and a purchase. When advertisements allow a viewer to purchase a product or service by pressing on an icon in the ad itself, the distinction between ads and purchases becomes blurred. As a result, pricing is likely to evolve into much more of a direct-marketing model, where the advertiser pays based on the volume of purchases generated by an ad rather than the number of hits or even clicks for more information. In one recent example, CD Now, a vendor of music CDs, agreed to pay a site featuring its advertisements a commission based on purchases generated from its banner ads.

As virtual communities become a forum for transactions and not simply advertising, the virtual community organizer becomes positioned to charge the vendor a "commission" on each transaction. These commissions now run somewhere between 2 percent and 10 percent of the purchase value. As transaction volume increases, there is the further possibility of the virtual community's "squeezing out" traditional intermediaries like retailers and distributors so that members can deal directly with producers of goods or services. In this case, the virtual community organizer may be able to capture additional revenue by splitting between itself and the producer the margin previously enjoyed by the intermediary.

Finally, another source of revenue theoretically available to the virtual community organizer is from the sale or "rental" of member usage or transaction profiles to third parties. While there are many precedents for such revenue streams in traditional businesses (such as the sale of magazine subscriber lists or direct mail customer lists), we have ignored this revenue stream in our own economic modeling of virtual community revenues. This "trading" in member profiles could significantly undermine the relationship between the community organizer and its members and, as a result, jeopardize the community's ability to develop advertising and transaction revenue streams that over time would dwarf the economic value of trading in member profiles. Even if a community organizer chooses to trade profiles, privacy protection laws may limit this activity, as is the case even today in many European countries.

We believe that aspiring organizers projecting potential revenues for their community will be best served by focusing exclusively on revenue generated from advertising and transactions. This avoids reliance on subscription or usage fees, which have undesirable dampening effects on member acquisition. Services like America Online and The Well have been able to build up significant subscriber bases while charging a combination of subscription and usage fees (minimum annual fees of $120 and $180, respectively), but the experience of companies trying to do this on the Internet has to date been discouraging. *USA Today* attempted to charge a $15/month subscription fee for access to its Internet site when it launched the site in early 1995, but it did not see significant growth in membership until after it dropped the subscription fee entirely later in the year. Perhaps one reason home users of the Internet have been so resistant to member fees is that they must pay roughly $240 per year in fees to an Internet service provider simply to access the Internet.

This resistance to member fees is likely to be much lower in the business-to-business arena, where Internet access is typically funded by the company and the economic value of participation in communities can be much more easily quantified. For example, Nets, Inc., charges vendors thousands of dollars in registration fees to participate in its electronic market (while buyers, at least for now, pay nothing). Even in the consumer arena, certain communities, such as those devoted to sufferers of a particular disease, may be able to charge membership fees given the clear value of participation and the likely reluctance of members to be exposed to much advertising or to engage in significant transaction activity as part of the community.

To understand these revenue sources better, let's take the example of a hypothetical virtual community that is successful in serving the consumer traveler in the United States. Assume the organizer of this community starts operation at the beginning of 1997 with an initial investment fund of $15 million and then aggressively builds the community to optimize revenue and net present value. Figure 3-2 indicates that the organizer of such a community, if successful, could reasonably generate approximately $90 million in revenue in its fifth year of operation and about $620 million in its tenth year. (These revenue numbers are derived from an extensive computer model developed for use with clients. Subsequent figures and numbers in this chapter were also derived from this model.) Advertising revenues represent just over 75 percent of these earnings in year five and just under the same percentage in year ten. By year ten, the community is generating $170 million in travel commissions, which implies that (at a 5 percent commission rate) the community is generating more than $3.3 billion in travel transactions. Even at this rate, the community would represent less than 4 percent of the projected total spending on leisure travel (in both the virtual and the physical worlds) by year ten.

To provide some perspective, the revenue potential in the tenth year is about eight times the $78 million in revenue generated by *Travel & Leisure,* one of the largest travel specialty magazines, and more than two hundred times the revenue of an average travel agency office in the United States. The message: virtual communities, with their transactional capabilities and broad geographic reach, have the potential to generate significant revenue streams for their organizers.

Figure 3-2 Potential Revenue Growth for a Successful Travel Community

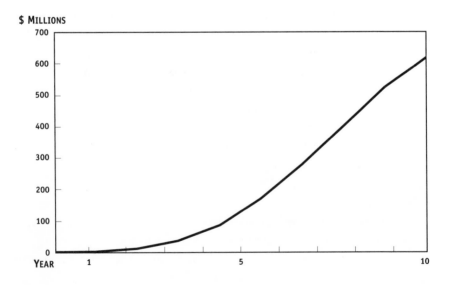

The proportion drawn from each revenue source will of course differ significantly depending on the distinctive focus of the community. Some communities, such as a designer clothing community, may be much more advertising intensive, while other communities, such as business-to-business, transaction-specific communities, will tend to be more transaction-commission intensive.

HOW THE DYNAMICS OF INCREASING RETURNS DRIVE REVENUE GROWTH

Now that we've examined where the revenues are likely to come from in a virtual community, we can look at the key factors influencing how fast these revenues will grow. In particular, we can look at a series of interacting and reinforcing virtuous cycles that, if understood, can be actively managed to accelerate and magnify revenue growth. Figure 3-3 presents an overview of these cycles, or loops. Each can be disaggregated into finer and finer levels of detail, as illustrated in figure 3-4, although even these representations are still highly simplified views of the complex interactions driving economic growth in the community.

The first of these loops is the *content attractiveness dynamic loop*. It reflects one of the key assumptions underlying the virtual community model—that member-generated content is a key source of content attractiveness and that content attractiveness in turn drives members to

Figure 3-3 Overview of the Dynamics of Increasing Returns

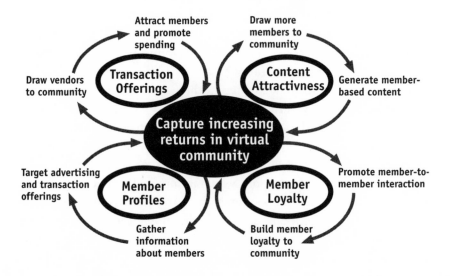

join and stay in a virtual community. Figure 3-4 shows the content at-tractiveness dynamic at work; for example, the accumulation of mem-ber-generated content will make the community more attractive and improve the effectiveness of marketing expenditures. What's important to remember is that this accumulation rate is driven by both the num-ber of members and the amount of time they spend on-line in the com-munity interacting with each other. So this loop is self-reinforcing: the more members a community has, the more member-generated content it is likely to accumulate and therefore the more members it will attract.

The *member loyalty dynamic loop* (also shown in figure 3-4), high-lights the role of key variables in driving membership churn (or turnover) and usage rates. For example, the more a community can pro-mote personal relationships between its members, the more loyal to the community members are likely to become, the more likely they are to participate in community forums, and the less likely they are to leave the community. Similarly, the more customized the interaction a com-munity offers (for example, software that has "learned" a member's preferences based on previous activity), the more loyal to the commu-nity members are likely to become. Once again, the self-reinforcing nature of the loop is evident: more loyalty generates more usage, more participation in community forums, and more personal relationships between members. This in turn generates more loyalty.

As members are drawn in and develop loyalty to the community, another powerful loop kicks in: the *member profile dynamic loop* (see fig-ure 3-4). This loop draws attention to the critical role member profiles play in generating economic value for the community. Its effectiveness hinges on key assumptions regarding the availability and deployment of robust technology for capturing information, something that is quite well developed in services like America Online but, by 1996, still in early development in the Internet arena. (This assumption will be addressed in more detail in chapter 8, where we discuss the strategy for deploying technology in the virtual community). Member profiles sig-nificantly enhance the ability to target advertising, which in turn strengthens the ability to increase click-through rates and to draw in even more advertisers. Member profiles also provide a basis for draw-ing in more appropriate vendors, which in turn will increase transaction activity. The increased transaction activity then serves to draw in even more vendors. These member profiles not only attract more appropri-ate vendors and advertisers, they help these vendors and advertisers to be more effective in reaching the right members. This in turn helps the community organizer to generate more revenue from transactions and advertising. Here, too, we see a self-reinforcing dynamic at play: more detailed member profiles draw in more advertisers and vendors and help them to be more effective in reaching their target, while the interaction of members with advertisers and vendors generates even more detailed member profiles, beginning the cycle all over again.

Finally, the *transaction offerings dynamic loop* (also profiled in figure 3-4) captures the reinforcing effects of expanding the range of products and services offered in the virtual community. As the range of products and services offered increases, more members are likely to join the community, while the members already in the community typically develop a greater willingness to engage in transactions. These developments in turn increase the attractiveness of the community to vendors, which draws more vendors in and increases the number of products and services available for sale. More product and service offerings lead to more transaction activity, which leads to more offerings, and the cycle begins again.

All four of these dynamic loops are examples of increasing returns achieved through network effects. The aggregation of members, member-generated content, member profiles, and vendors is an increasing returns game. The more a community has, the more incentive others have to join, and therefore the more the community will get. The value of the "network" rises exponentially with the growth of network nodes.

Static versus dynamic revenue models

Understanding these loops is essential for aspiring community organizers looking to get a handle on what their virtual community investment will be worth ten years from now. After all, without understanding how quickly revenues streams are likely to grow, it's extremely difficult to put a valuation on a virtual community.

Static spreadsheets will see the tip and miss the iceberg.

In fact, the steepness of revenue growth over time and the magnitude of revenue generation are likely to be underestimated using conventional financial analysis techniques. Organizers who use these conventional techniques may end up vastly underestimating the potential of their virtual community investment and therefore either foregoing investment

Figure 3-4 A Closer Look at the Four Dynamics of Increasing Returns

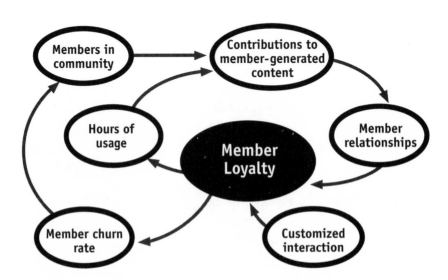

Figure 3-4 continued

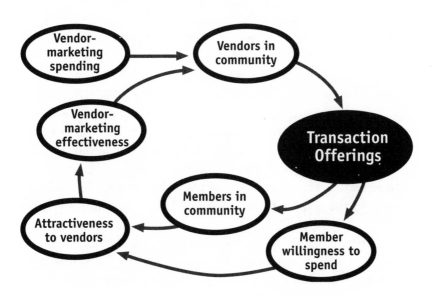

entirely or underinvesting and thereby increasing the risk of preemption and business failure.

The reason is that in the traditional valuation approach, "snapshots" of virtual community economics are taken on a spreadsheet for specific periods of time (that is, year one, year five, year ten). These snapshots are shaped by assumptions regarding key variables at each point in time. Without a history of virtual community performance, analogs for these variables must be found and tested for "plausibility." Because managers tend to be cautious about even straight-line growth projections into the future—and because few have had experience with the accelerating growth patterns of increasing returns businesses—we find that "plausible" assumptions tend to be systematically underestimated.

In contrast, a business dynamics approach forces aspiring organizers explicitly and systematically to identify and understand the self-reinforcing dynamic loops that operate in increasing returns businesses. As a result, by starting with the same assumptions in year one, the dynamic model of virtual community economics will typically yield much higher projections of revenue in following years.

To illustrate this point, consider our hypothetical virtual community targeting consumer travelers in the United States. Figure 3-5 contrasts a traditional approach to projecting revenue for this hypothetical community with a more dynamic approach that focuses on the effects of the kinds of self-reinforcing dynamic loops just discussed. As early as year five of the virtual community initiative, the traditional approach to revenue estimation yields a revenue projection only about one-fourth the size of the dynamic revenue projection, and by year ten the traditional approach has underestimated revenue potential by a factor of twenty-two relative to the dynamic approach.

Even if aspiring organizers understood the individual dynamic loops in operation in a virtual community, it is unlikely they would anticipate the cumulative effect of these dynamic loops as they interact with each other. It is a classic case of the whole being greater than the sum of the parts. While each dynamic loop is a powerful driver of economic performance on its own, figure 3-6 shows how their combined effect is far greater than the effect of any individual loop. Computer-based business dynamics models can capture and quantify the reinforcing effect of dynamic loops; static spreadsheet models cannot.

This is a key lesson of the business dynamics model: multiple dynamic loops act cumulatively on each other in ways that are hard to anticipate. For this reason, all of the loops must be tightly managed. Exclusive focus on only one or two is likely to result in a loss of economic value.

Implications for management

A community has a number of key economic assets that will fuel its growth. Chief among these assets are its members—not all of whom have equal value to a particular community.

Figure 3-5 A Static and Dynamic View of Projected Revenues ($ Millions)

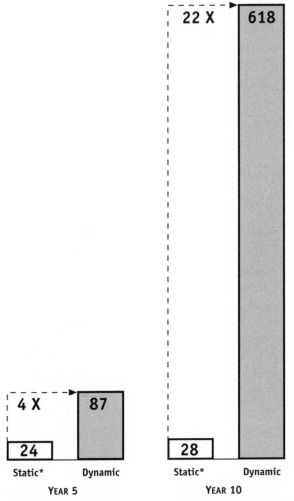

*Based on a straight-line projection starting with the same set of ingoing assumptions.

Targeting growth assets. By observing these dynamic loops in operation, the community organizer can begin to identify and focus on the key assets that drive growth. These are:

- Critical mass of members
- Critical mass of usage profiles
- Critical mass of advertisers/vendors
- Critical mass of transaction profiles
- Critical mass of transactions

In the early stages of community development, the goal is to accumulate the first growth asset—a critical mass of members. Much of the value of the community to members hinges on their ability to connect with others, and much of the economic value to the community organizer hinges on aggregating a critical mass of members of interest to relevant advertisers and vendors. A critical mass of members unleashes a series of other opportunities, the most important being the opportunity to aggregate usage profiles of members, which is the second major growth asset of the community. As we have seen, a critical mass of usage profiles is essential for driving the member profile dynamic loop, with its reinforcing effects on advertising and transaction activity.

Figure 3-6 The Cumulative Effect of Dynamic Loops ($ Millions)

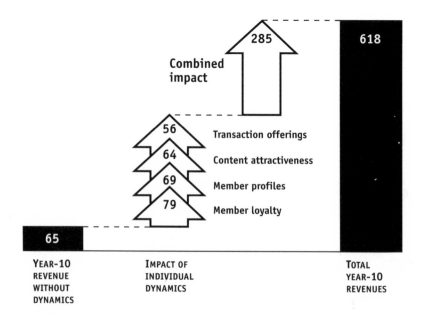

YEAR-10 REVENUE WITHOUT DYNAMICS	**IMPACT OF INDIVIDUAL DYNAMICS**	**TOTAL YEAR-10 REVENUES**

(Owing to the absence of adequate information capture technology, this is where many Internet-based communities are stalled today.)

The third growth asset involves aggregation of advertisers and vendors within the community. Usage profiles help to draw these commercial participants into the community, and the resulting increase in advertising and transaction activity not only helps to enrich the usage profiles but also starts to generate member transaction profiles. Now the community organizer begins to learn which members are heavy on-line purchasers and how they are segmented in terms of the kinds of products and services they buy. This information makes up the fourth growth asset, which in turn helps to accumulate the information necessary to build up the fifth and final growth asset: a critical mass of transactions occurring within the community. The more a community organizer knows about members in terms of their transaction activity, the more effective the organizer will be in merchandising and facilitating even more transactions. At some point, many communities are likely to represent a significant share of the transactions that occur within particular transaction categories, not only relative to other virtual communities and on-line sites but relative to transactions that occur in physical space as well. This creates the potential for a number of further business initiatives, which are described later in this chapter in the section "Longer-Term Sources of Value Creation."

These growth assets will not be equally valuable across all communities, and in some communities one or more may be irrelevant. As we have mentioned, business-to-business virtual communities are likely to be more transaction intensive than consumer-oriented virtual communities, which are likely to be more advertising intensive. Thus, for transaction-intensive communities, the accumulation of a critical mass of vendors, transaction profiles, and transaction activity will have much more value than it will for more advertising-intensive communities, where asset values will be much more concentrated in usage profiles and the aggregation of advertisers.

While these community growth assets may reach critical mass in a sequential manner, community organizers will try to develop them much more in parallel, as presented in figure 3-7. To some degree, especially as advertising moves to more of a charge-per-click-through approach, the community organizer may be able to attract a significant number of advertisers simply by aggregating a critical mass of members without waiting for a critical mass of usage profiles to accumulate.

Similarly, a business-to-business, transaction-oriented community may be able to build a critical mass of transactions before it has accumulated detailed usage or transaction profiles of its members. Given the considerable lead times involved in developing some of these growth assets (deployment of data capture technology and accumulation of usage profiles, for example), community organizers need to begin to build each growth asset as soon as it is economically feasible.

Managing member evolution. Since building a critical mass of members is such an important threshold event for community organizers, it is worth spending a little more time developing some of the economics of community membership. Even though they don't appear anywhere on the balance sheet, members are in a very real sense the key economic asset of a community.

Three points are important. First, community members are likely to evolve in terms of their role and economic contribution to the community. Second, not all members are equal in terms of their economic potential for the community. Third, as in all service businesses, some key variables significantly shape overall economic performance: the

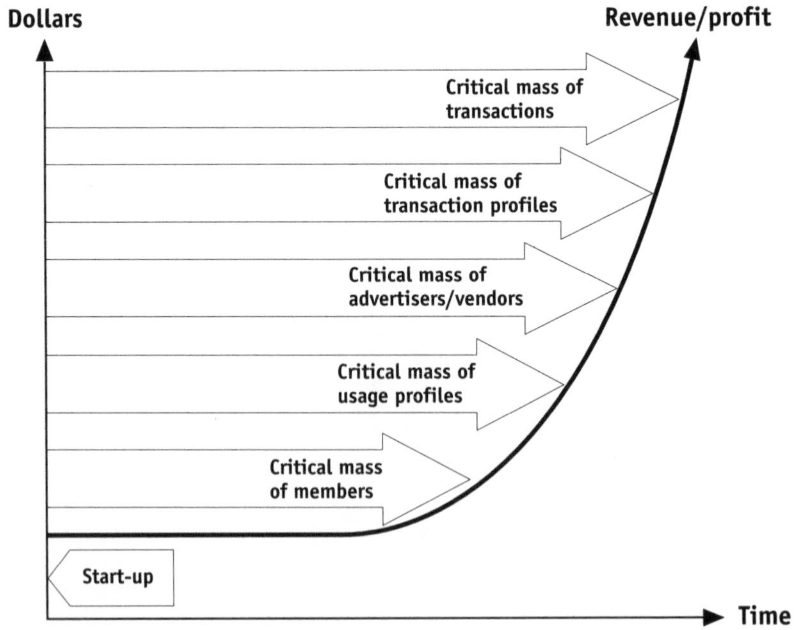

Figure 3-7 Development Milestones of Virtual Communities

cost of member acquisition, the net profit generated by each member during his or her time as a member, and the average churn rate, which determines the average length of membership.

On the first point, the evolving role and contribution of community members, the community organizer should expect to support four stages of development. (Figure 3-8 highlights the four stages and some of the levers used to sustain them.) As with most products and services, the first challenge is to interest people in trying out your offering; if no one tries it, no one's going to get hooked into using it for any period of time. Once people do join the community, the next challenge is to get them to increase their participation. Ideally, they should visit often and spend a lot of time on each visit. As members increase their participation, the community organizer will want to build their loyalty and make sure they stay; members shouldn't be lost because they lose interest or find a more attractive community offering somewhere else. Finally, the commercially driven community organizer will want to capture value from members. Depending on the commercial focus of the community, this value could take the form of advertising revenues, transaction commissions, or fees paid directly by the member.

This notion of a "typical" path of member development underscores the importance of the second point: not all community members are equal in terms of their economic potential to the community, and the nature of their economic contribution can differ substantially. Typically, members enter into a virtual community as "browsers" testing

Figure 3-8 Four Stages of Member Development

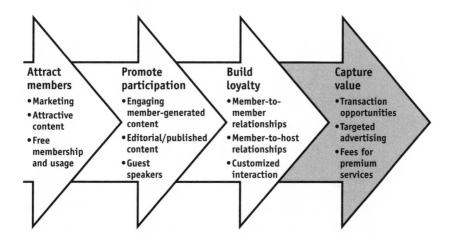

the waters. Some will stay, but many won't, and those who do are generally characterized by low usage rates. Browsers are of little economic value to a community unless they shift into one of the other categories. One role they can play is to spread a positive "buzz" about the community in other forums on the network and thereby help to bring in more browsers, some of whom may become active members.

Over time, browsers tend to become either "builders" or "users." Builders are those members who are most passionate about the community and most active in contributing member-generated content. They spend a lot of time in the community and, in many respects, become the connective tissue that binds it together. The community organizer will capture some direct monetary value from builders because they tend to spend a lot of time in the community and might be interesting targets for advertisers. Even more important, this category of member often generates enormous indirect value by fueling the growth of member-generated content. For this reason, community organizers may actually pay builders to reward them for their contribution (and to encourage even more).

When Stewart Brand established The Well, he carefully targeted and recruited a core membership of hackers and journalists by offering them free access (waiving the $15/month base subscription fee). He believed they would be active contributors to The Well's various forums and would in turn bring in many other members. Brand was correct. The early success of The Well was explained in large part by the early presence of this core of builders.

"Users," sometimes called lurkers, are people who spend more time in the community than browsers and benefit from its information but who neither contribute significantly to member-generated content nor actively purchase products or services. Because of the time they spend in the community, the community organizer may be able to capture rich usage profiles of them and use this information to attract appropriate advertisers. Where advertising is not a major element in the community, this member may have less value than those in some of the other categories.

Finally, "buyers" are those members who actively purchase products and services within the community. They certainly generate substantial transaction commissions, and they may also be significant drivers of advertising revenue. Depending on the importance of transaction activity in the community, these members may be among the most valuable of all.

Of course, in real life—or at least in virtual space—members are likely to represent a complex mix of elements from all four categories described. The community organizer's challenge is to understand in some detail the economic role played by and the economic value contributed by each member—and to be creative in identifying ways to enhance this contribution over time. The very different economic value each of these member categories has to offer is clearly visible in our hypothetical travel virtual community. In this model, builders are the most valuable, generating $305 in revenue apiece in year ten, compared with $260 in revenues from buyers and $175 from users.

The proportion of these four categories of members in a community is likely to vary over time. Since the travel community is projected to grow at an aggressive pace, browsers tend to dominate membership at any point in time. One objective of the community organizer should be to convert browsers rapidly into any of the other three higher revenue-generating categories.

In general, community organizers will want to acquire new members at the lowest possible cost, realize substantial profit per member, and keep each member as long as possible. One of the major challenges of the Internet today is the amount of churn around Web sites. People come and go, but they rarely stay. Surfing rules.

Even well-established on-line services like America Online experience substantial churn, estimated to be on the order of 30 percent to 40 percent per year. These kinds of churn rates are particularly troublesome when substantial amounts are spent on member acquisition. Depending on how one interprets AOL's accounting practices, the service spends anywhere from $40 to $90 to acquire a new member. The fact that the average member leaves after a relatively short period of time is one reason why America Online, despite substantial subscriber fees, is unable to achieve higher profitability.

Loyalty pays. Our economic model of the consumer travel community suggests that member acquisition cost could decline from $25 in year one to $9 in year ten, based on such factors as increasing member loyalty and content attractiveness. Even an aggressive travel community might have substantially lower member acquisition costs than America Online. This is partly because the marketing of a travel community would be much more focused. AOL wants everyone; the travel community wants only the active leisure traveler. It is also because AOL has—at least thus far—decided to deliver start-up disks to the target member (reflecting its proprietary network focus) rather than assume that members will obtain the necessary software and then get service from a specialized access provider, as a community on the Internet might. The model suggests that churn rates could drop from 32 percent in year one to 13 percent in year ten. Net profit per member ramps up steadily over the life of the community, reaching roughly $80 per year by year ten.

Once again, traditional static valuation techniques will get a community organizer into trouble. By ignoring the dynamic loop effects operating within the community, a static valuation model systematically underestimates the value of individual members. This in turn leads the community organizer to underinvest in member acquisition and in measures to reduce churn rates.

The static valuation model misses an important aspect of member value. Typically, such models take a snapshot of the average profit generated by a member in one year and multiply by the average number of years a member stays with the community. What this approach misses is the additional profit likely to be generated by each member in future years as a result of the growth of the overall community and the reinforcing effect this has on the activity of the individual member in question. As the community grows larger, that individual will have more opportunities to interact with others, which is likely to increase member-generated content and add more detail to that individual's usage profile. This in turn increases advertising and transaction opportunities. Increased interaction with others may also directly stimulate more purchases, as members "sell" each other on the benefit of certain products.

The bottom line is that each member of the virtual community is a key driver of economic value. In the hypothetical community we modeled, the average revenue generated by each member grows from $7 in year one to $159 in year ten. Those who understand the true value of these members and the sources of that value will be best positioned to grow virtual communities into large and profitable businesses.

HOW THE DYNAMICS OF INCREASING RETURNS IMPROVE PROFITABILITY

Increasing returns help to accelerate revenue growth. They also help to drive down unit costs over time. These cost effects combine with strong revenue growth to yield substantial cash flow on a net present value basis and sizable shareholder value.

Cost dynamics of a virtual community

In shifting from revenues to costs, three key points should be kept in mind. First, the investment required to start a virtual community is not substantial, at least by the standards of a large company. Second, the primary operating costs in a virtual community have little to do with technology and much more to do with acquisition of members and of participating advertisers and vendors. Third, many of these operating costs are subject to the same kind of increasing returns dynamics discussed above, which leads to lower unit costs over time.

Two million dollars can get you in the game — today, that is.

In terms of investment, our consumer travel community model assumes that the community organizer starts with $15 million of cash in the bank and pursues a highly leveraged entry strategy (outlined in chapter 6). The organizer pursues a preemptive member acquisition campaign, successfully building the community from about 80,000 members in the first full year of operation to about 900,000 members by year five (roughly equivalent to the paid circulation of *Travel & Leisure* magazine). With the exception of an additional infusion of $5 million in capital in year three, the virtual community is essentially self-funding, despite substantial growth.

Figure 3-9 indicates that the up-front costs of setting up the community—which consist largely of capital expenditures for the initial community platform and development efforts by a small team to put together the initial community site—are quite small, totaling about $1–2 million. Once again, this assumes a highly leveraged start-up strategy on the Internet where the initial community offer consists of some basic directory services and forums for member-generated content. The specific amount and nature of the start-up expense will certainly vary depending both on the distinctive focus of the virtual community and the entry strategy. In most cases, we believe the start-up expenses should not vary by more than $2 million above the model estimate if the community organizer pursues the leveraged entry strategy recommended in chapter 6.

Potential operating costs for the consumer travel community are summarized in figure 3-10 for years one and five. Technology-related costs, consisting of facilities operations and data gathering and customization expenses, actually represent a relatively small, and rapidly declining, portion of the total operating cost (declining from 35 percent of costs in year one to 12 percent in year five). Even these percentages are overstated, since a substantial portion of the expense in the data-gathering category is for analysts who develop the usage and transaction profiles used to attract advertisers and vendors to the community.

These technology-related costs are overwhelmed by member acquisition costs, advertiser acquisition costs, and content-related costs, which collectively grow from 61 percent to 66 percent of total operating costs over the five-year period. In most communities, vendor acquisition costs would probably be more significant than in the consumer travel community, where an affiliation with a single computer reservation system can deliver the full range of airlines and an assortment of other travel-related services. The net result is that virtual communities are largely driven by expense categories typical of traditional, nontechnology companies. In short, this is not a technology play. There is no reason to believe technology companies will be advantaged in any way in managing these kinds of expenses.

These nontechnology costs all benefit from unit cost reductions over time, which are driven by the same dynamic loops described above. Until saturation of the available market becomes an issue, member acquisition costs are likely to decline over time for leading virtual communities as they pull ahead of their competitors in terms of the range of members, content, and vendors they offer. Our travel community model suggests that the cost to acquire each new member could decline by almost 65 percent over the ten years, if the community is properly managed. Decreased churn further magnifies the economic value of this effect, since the organizer spends less to keep the member longer.

Similarly, we anticipate greater marketing effectiveness in the model in terms of acquiring new advertisers. The community is able to attract advertisers more readily once it has an accumulation of members and their usage profiles, as well as growing experience with targeting ads. This in turn leads to lower costs to acquire each new advertiser.

Figure 3-9 Start-Up Costs for the Consumer Travel Community

	Estimated Cost ($ Millions)	Percentage of Total
Initial content • Editorial • Published	$0.3–0.6	30%
Technical setup • Servers • Lines • Site development • PCs • System operators	0.4–0.8	40
Data gathering/customized interaction • Hardware/software • Database setup • Analysts	0.2–0.4	20
Staff and general • Management • Customer service • Administrators • Advertising sales • Customer/vendor marketing • Office space/equipment	0.1–0.2	10
Total	$1.0–2.0	100%

Figure 3-10 Cost Structure of the Consumer Travel Community

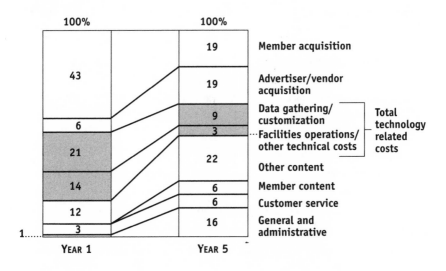

Content acquisition should also benefit. A leading community with a large membership already in place and a detailed understanding of its members should be able to mobilize a much broader range of published content in its community at far lower cost than a smaller community. In this business, the big not only get bigger, they also get more profitable, riding a steadily declining unit cost curve for major cost categories.

Of course, the specific cost structures that evolve in a virtual community over time will reflect strategy and operational choices made by the community organizer. The sensitivity of virtual community revenues and profits to specific decisions in terms of spending more or less in particular programs such as advertiser acquisition can be demonstrated by the economic model. Figure 3-11 illustrates this kind of sensitivity analysis for the consumer travel community for investment changes made in the second year of operation (1998). So, for example, an additional investment in acquiring vendors made in year two will eventually yield twenty times the amount in revenues over the ten-year period, while the same additional investment made instead in acquiring members will yield a ninefold return in revenue terms. One of the lessons to be learned from this sensitivity modeling is that the impact of spending more or less varies not only by spending category but by year and by scenario assumptions (for instance, high growth,

Figure 3-11 Impact of Investment Decisions on Revenue

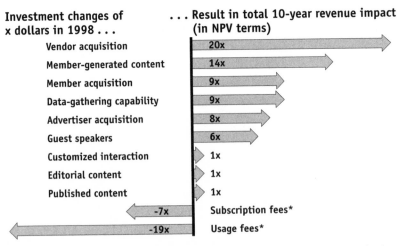

*Calculated as the ratio of other revenue lost versus incremental fee revenue gained.

lower investment). A cutback in data-gathering capability made in an early year will have far greater effect on the growth and profitability potential of the community than a similar cutback made several years later.

Cash flow over time

Driven by accelerating revenue growth and declining unit costs in major cost categories, virtual community initiatives are likely to generate substantial pretax operating cash over time. Figure 3-12 summarizes the annual pretax operating cash flow profile of the consumer travel community. After three years of negative cash flow, the community turns cash positive and by year ten is generating more than $300 million in annual cash flow. Figure 3-12 also shows the cumulative pretax operating cash flow profile of the same community. The community goes cash negative to the cumulative amount of $20 million in year three, then goes cash positive on a cumulative basis by year five and generates a projected $930 million in cumulative cash flow over the ten-year period. The net present value of this cumulative cash flow can be substantial: at a 10 percent discount rate, the net present value of cumulative pretax operating cash flow over ten years could be $425

Figure 3-12 Pretax Operating Cash Flow ($ Millions)

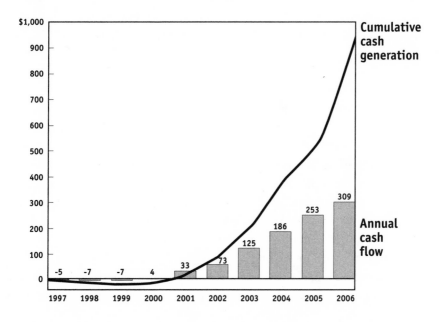

million for the consumer travel community. This is certainly a sizable incentive for even very large companies to seek to organize their own virtual communities. It is a fortune awaiting smaller entrepreneurs.

Shareholder value

The combination of accelerating growth and improving profitability should have a magnifying impact on the potential shareholder value created by a virtual community. Based on high profitability and a projected growth rate of 20 percent going forward, it is likely that such a virtual community initiative would support a multiple of 30x on earnings in year ten. This suggests that the shareholder value of the travel community enterprise in year ten would be more than $4 billion. Given this kind of value creation opportunity, a broad range of entrants will be crowding into this business.

LONGER-TERM SOURCES OF VALUE CREATION

Some readers may find our suggestion that a virtual community might command a multiple as high as 30x year-ten earnings to be a bit aggressive. In response, we would point out that the previous discussion of the economics of virtual communities excludes a number of elements that could represent a significant upside over and above the financial results just reviewed. Since these elements are more speculative, we have hesitated to quantify them, but they should be identified and understood as part of any effort to evaluate entry into the virtual community business.

Transaction share: The long-term opportunity

Once a virtual community captures a significant share of the transactions occurring within any transaction category (the fifth growth asset described above), substantial opportunities are likely to exist for the community organizer to reshape broader industry structures. For example, if the community starts to represent a significant share of the transaction activity within given transaction categories, the community organizer may have sufficient scale and bargaining power to displace traditional intermediaries and to connect producers of goods and services directly with members.

The nature and size of this opportunity will hinge on many factors, including the number of producers and traditional intermediaries, the share of transactions that occurs on-line, the profit made by traditional intermediaries, and the specific role these intermediaries play. (For example, how much of the value is in bringing many vendors together for the customer or in providing scale in logistics operations or expertise in configuring complex systems to meet individual customer needs?)

In our consumer travel example, the virtual community might ultimately displace conventional travel agents for all types of travel arrangements and even develop a computer reservation system of its own. Travel agencies in the United States today are experiencing declining operating margins. Travel agencies are not highly concentrated (although concentration trends are increasing), and the producers of travel services other than transportation itself (hotels and tour companies, for instance) are highly fragmented. The consumer travel virtual community might therefore capture a significant share of the travel agency operating margin if it chooses to disintermediate the agency. Since fulfillment of travel transactions does not require handling of bulky physical goods, the travel community might assume all the functions of a traditional travel intermediary without having to develop significant additional skills or facilities.

Beyond disintermediation, the travel community with a significant share of transaction activity can leverage scale on behalf of its members. For example, the travel community might purchase large blocks of airline tickets or cruise ship tickets at a substantial discount and then pass some of these savings on to members by reselling the tickets.

More fundamentally, the travel community might become a catalyst for the development of very different reverse-market pricing structures. What would a reverse market in travel look like? In such a world, the traveler would notify vendors of its travel plans and seek bids for specific elements of the travel package. For example, a traveler seeking to vacation in Japan might ask airlines to bid for the airline travel component, hotels in Kyoto to bid for the accommodations component, and various tour companies to bid for the opportunity to provide appropriate tours.

How would such transactions be priced? As in the Nets, Inc., market space, vendors might be required to pay a substantial registration fee simply for the privilege of participating in this market space. Members might pay an auction fee to the community organizer for orchestrating the bidding process to ensure that the broadest range of appropriate vendors are mobilized to bid, and then the winning vendor might pay a transaction commission based on the value of the transaction. Pricing structures for reverse markets are highly speculative but, at least in some scenarios, could represent an attractive upside for virtual communities relative to the more conventional pricing approaches in use today.

Platform for growth: options for future value creation

Beyond the revenue streams identified in the economic model above, a consumer travel community might be positioned to address a broad range of other business opportunities. Within the travel community itself, there may be additional revenue streams available over time. For example, we have not assumed the community organizer charges members for anything—all revenues are generated by advertisers and/or vendors. As the community matures, the organizer may be in a better position to charge subscription fees or premiums for delivery of specific content (for instance, charging for the downloading of a map showing the best restaurants in Kyoto). The community organizer may also capture and sell to its members reviews of vendor activities to help members make better choices (for instance, indicating which hotels in the Caribbean have received the most repeat bookings from members of the travel community).

The community organizer may also be able to attract a broader advertiser base to reach its members than we have assumed in our model. In the model, we assume that the relevant pool of advertising revenues is the amount spent on travel-related advertising in the United States today. However, the membership of an on-line travel community is likely to have attractive demographics (higher income, younger households) that would appeal to a broad range of advertisers beyond the providers of travel-related products and services.

Also, we have limited the definition of the travel market on several dimensions. We assume the virtual community largely targets consumer travel originating in the United States (we assumed the community might also be able to target a portion—about 10 percent—of the business travel market where the purchase decision is closely related to leisure travel). Once this market is developed, wouldn't there be natural opportunities to expand the scope of the community to include a much broader range of business travel? One could imagine small businesses using such a service extensively for business travel, particularly if the virtual community can deliver services at a lower cost than conventional sources.

Similarly, why restrict the scope over time to travel originating in the United States? One of the powers of the network is its capacity to reach people regardless of geography. A member could log on from Australia just as readily as from Dallas. Why not serve the travel needs of all English-speaking people around the world? As language translation capability improves, one could imagine the travel community reaching out across the globe, regardless of language spoken. Netscape already permits users of its browser software to select the language for displaying Web sites (although this assumes Web site developers have translated their content into the selected languages). Providing a travel community for everyone around the world opens up the possibility of some very interesting arbitrage opportunities, created by selected availability on fares in certain countries. For example, an Australian seeking domestic air travel reservations in the United States could pay less by purchasing these tickets in the United States—or in the virtual community—than by purchasing them in Australia. (This, of course, raises interesting issues for regulatory policies.)

Finally, within the travel sphere, we have assumed that the target membership of the virtual community is drawn only from those who are on-line and who have demonstrated a strong interest in travel, defined either as reading a travel-related magazine or as taking frequent leisure trips. Over time, one might reasonably expect more casual leisure travelers to be attracted to this community, both for the convenience of having such a rich set of travel-related resources and for the potential price advantages driven by the scale of the community as a whole. While such casual travelers might not become active, contributing members of the community and might not even visit on a regular basis, the commissions earned on their travel bookings could become significant.

The ability to reach a broader travel audience might be enhanced by thinking aggressively about expanding the franchise of the travel community back into physical space. In much the same way that the Gardner brothers, founders of Motley Fool, have now written a best-selling book on financial investments, one could imagine a travel virtual community expanding its reach by publishing a travel magazine (on paper, no less) or launching a direct marketing effort using "snail mail" to reach potential travelers who are not yet on-line.

Even more speculatively, a travel community might be well positioned to diversify into related virtual community initiatives as it develops a critical mass of members who begin to display other interests or needs besides travel. For example, one could imagine a significant number of college students joining a travel community. As this group becomes larger, it might launch a travel subcommunity that addresses their specific needs and interests (through a process of building "fractal depth," described in more detail in chapter 5). Within that travel subcommunity targeting college students, it might become apparent that members would value a broader range of services aimed at their needs as college students (for example, ratings of colleges, job search bulletin boards). This subcommunity could become a seedbed for establishing a community that more broadly addresses the needs of these members beyond just travel (through a process of building "fractal breadth," also described in more detail in chapter 5).

The bottom line is that a consumer travel virtual community represents a robust platform for growth, generating a broad range of growth options, many of which cannot even be anticipated, much less quantified, at the outset. The challenge for the community organizer is to reflect the value of these potential growth options in making investment decisions at the outset and then to pursue these options aggressively as they emerge.

NEAR-TERM ECONOMIC CHALLENGES

The substantial long-term value creation potential of virtual communities notwithstanding, organizers of virtual communities are likely to face significant near-term economic challenges on both the revenue side and the cost side. They will be driven by two forces: competitive dynamics and technology evolution. Navigation of these near-term challenges by the community organizer will shape in significant ways the entry strategies explored in chapter 6. But the economic message is clear: those who enter the virtual community business expecting a quick return on investment are likely to be severely disappointed.

Revenue pressures

In a nutshell, the dilemma for the virtual community organizer is that the most accessible revenue sources in the near term will be the least attractive from the viewpoint of driving growth. On the other hand, the revenue sources that are most attractive are likely to be beyond the reach of the community organizer in the early years of community formation. The result will be limited revenue generation from the virtual community in the near term.

As discussed earlier, one revenue source immediately available to the community organizer is member fees (especially subscription or usage fees), which can be charged from the first day. However, charging member fees is likely to slow growth of membership substantially. That in turn could delay

Why the revenues you can get are not the revenues you want.

readiness to tap into other attractive revenue streams: advertising and transaction commissions. It could also expose the community organizer to competitive threats from more aggressive competitors pursuing pre-emptive member acquisition strategies and therefore offering free access to their community.

In contrast, while the virtual community organizer would love to be able to tap into advertising and transaction commission revenue streams from the outset, these will both take time to materialize. The problem is that it is very hard to sell advertising for a community with few, if any, members about which little is known. Advertising spending on the Internet has tended to be concentrated in the high-traffic Web sites. In 1995, for instance, the top ten Web sites captured 35 percent of all advertising spending and the top fifty sites captured 70 percent. The community organizer must deliver either a lot of traffic or a deep understanding of a more limited number of members, both of which take time to accumulate.

Transaction commissions depend both on the number of members as well as the number of vendors actively participating in the community (if the member clicks on a vendor icon and is immediately "transported" to a vendor's Web site, it will be much more difficult to capture a transaction commission than if the vendor's products or services are actually offered for sale in the virtual community environment). Winning vendor participation will not be easy, especially at the outset. With few potential customers (most of whom are poorly understood by the community organizer) combined with the concern over a new intermediary coming between the vendor and its customers, many vendors are likely to wait on the sidelines, at least at the outset, until a critical mass of members and usage profiles can be aggregated.

Adding to these challenges are some near-term technical realities. As discussed in chapter 8, the Internet (as of 1996) is not yet a commerce friendly environment. Key technologies in such areas as usage information capture, payment systems, and authentication are not yet broadly deployed, although substantial sums are being invested to address these issues. Therefore, much of the advertising and transaction commission potential remains beyond the reach of the virtual community on the Internet. Virtual communities emerging in such on-line services as America Online are in a better position with regard to these issues in the near term, but, as indicated in chapter 8, participation in on-line services creates its own set of concerns.

The net result: revenue generation by virtual communities in the near term is likely to be quite limited.

Cost pressures

Limited revenue generation might not be so bad on its own, but it is coupled with substantial near-term cost pressures. The result could be a near-term margin squeeze that is very painful, if not fatal, for the aspiring community organizer.

As we argue in chapter 6, virtual community organizers will need to pursue highly leveraged strategies by aggressively mobilizing other people's resources to serve their ends. Even with such leveraged strategies, however, the community organizer will be under enormous pressure to spend aggressively on member acquisition, especially in the first several years. This pressure will be both economic—driven by the desire to accumulate a critical mass of members and to unleash the dynamic loops described earlier—and competitive, driven by concern over the need to preempt competitors and, if possible, discourage them from entering at all. This competitive pressure is very real, and those who invest aggressively in member acquisition in the near term are likely to be significantly advantaged in the longer term.

The implication for community organizers is clear: take a deep breath, focus investment on preemptive member acquisition, and set realistic expectations about break-evens and payback periods. (Also, make certain that cash reserves are consistent with these expectations.) The early years of virtual community formation are likely to fulfill the words of a memorable Chinese curse: "May you live in interesting times."

EARLY ENTRANTS WILL GAIN THE FIELD

The same forces that make virtual communities an attractive long-term economic opportunity also create an imperative for early action. Those who aspire to play the role of community organizer or owner will need to move quickly and aggressively to increase the likelihood of becoming the first to aggregate a critical mass of members in a target area. Those who wait in the mistaken hope that uncertainties will "clear up" or that successful early entrants can be acquired are likely to find themselves in for a rude awakening. Increasing returns suggest that late entry will certainly be the most expensive option and may become so expensive that it is either prohibitive or at least unattractive, given the enormous up-front investment required and the difficulty of earning an adequate return on that investment.

Investment requirements escalate

Here's the catch: A low barrier to entry business now is almost certain to build insurmountable barriers to entry over the next five years. These barriers to entry take a variety of forms: unique assets accumulated by early entrants, switching barriers for members, factor cost increases, and scale and scope economies. The result will be to send the price of entry beyond the reach of most, if not all, potential players.

Unique assets accumulate. Virtual communities today start out on a relatively level playing field. The technology is broadly available to all, published content and vendors are likely to be accessible to all, communication forums are still at a relatively early stage of development, usage and transaction profiles are not yet highly developed, and few members have yet aggregated in available communities. No one has yet accumulated unique assets that differentiate one community from another in a compelling way and that must be replicated for a new entrant to be successful.

Fast-forward several years. By this time, virtual communities are in full swing in all the obvious categories. Aggressive member acquisition strategies have yielded their expected result: a critical mass of members participates in the leading communities, populated and active bulletin boards and chat areas are accumulating usage profiles, and as a result the communities are learning more and more about who their members are.

Established players have by now accumulated some unique assets that significantly differentiate their communities. First and foremost, they have members, a key asset relative to later entrants. Our economic model on the consumer travel community suggests that an aggressive organizer could acquire almost 400,000 members by the end of the third year of operation. Moreover, established communities have specific members with distinct identities who are unlikely to be active across multiple other communities within the same category. So, for example, if I want to interact with another passionate and well-informed traveler whom I had previously encountered in a travel community (call him Alan Fairgate), I am likely to find him active only on the bulletin boards and chat rooms of the specific community he has joined. A new entrant cannot create a clone of Alan Fairgate.

Second, their memberships will have a higher proportion of builders and buyers than a newcomer. It takes time to convert the browser.

Third, established organizers have accumulated significant amounts of member-generated content from their bulletin boards and chat areas that are unique to their communities. If I want access to that content, I must participate in that community. Also, because established players have accumulated large numbers of members, it is likely that this member-generated content has become quite deep and specific. In our consumer travel example, there would be a detailed archive of contributions on scuba-diving vacation destinations and another archive on wine-tasting trips. This is over and above the standard travel guides published on such topics. What source of "published" content can match the richness and specificity of these archives? What offer can the new entrant make to compensate for its lack of this information? How much of an investment and how much lead time will it take to deliver on that offer?

Check out Motley Fool on America Online and explore the diversity of bulletin boards already available, organized by type of industry, specific company, and type of investment strategy. Let the accumulation process advance another couple of years and then imagine yourself as a prospective community organizer seeking to address the needs of personal investors. What would you do to match the richness of unique material already available?

Fourth, established organizers will have accumulated detailed usage and perhaps transaction profiles of their members. They will know how much time they spend in the community, with whom they interact, what their interests are, and, in many cases, what kinds of products or services they have purchased. Once again, this information will be unique to the community that captured it. If an advertiser or vendor wants to target members with certain profiles, it will need to do business with the community organizer to leverage the value of that information. How would a new entrant with few members and even less information about them compete for advertiser spending or vendor time and attention?

Three years from now virtual communities will no longer be undifferentiated start-ups. The leaders will be well-developed commercial enterprises with a range of unique assets that give them powerful differentiation, from the perspective of potential new members as well as that of potential advertisers and vendors. Overcoming this differentiation will take significant investment and lead time, and even then it may not be possible.

Barriers to new allegiances get higher. Not only will established entrants have the advantage of strong differentiation to attract prospective new members, they will also probably have built substantial barriers to members transferring their allegiance to a different community. If that occurs, new entrants could find themselves locked out from much of the available market.

Perhaps the most significant, and yet most subtle, barriers to switching communities are the relationships that members develop within them. Those who become active in the communication forums of a community begin to get to know and trust the input of other members. Professor Alan Fairgate may have been particularly helpful to me in planning my last archaeological vacation not only because he shared my passion for archaeology but also because he had been to most of the archaeological sites I am interested in and seems to share my preferences regarding food and accommodations. I now consult with him every time I plan a vacation. How willing might I be to shift to a newly organized travel community if Alan remains in the community we are both in now? Alan has become a major switching barrier for me, and there are ten others like him in the community that I have come to trust and rely on for helping me plan my vacation travel. Either we all switch or none of us switch.

One of the reasons there is such a high churn rate today within on-line offerings is that few on-line initiatives have focused on developing the moderated communication forums in which these personal relationships can develop. Those few who have developed such forums have generally done so recently, and there has not been enough time for these relationships to form.

Even more subtly, members are likely to establish significant, trusting relationships with virtual community organizers. Back in the travel community, I have come to rely on the community organizer for quality assurance, both with regard to the members I interact with and the resources (content, vendors, and so forth) presented to me. If it is available in this community, I know it is of high quality, and this saves me an enormous amount of time and potential confusion. Also, communities will be in a position to capture detailed information about members, and members will need to be able to trust the community organizer not to abuse this information.

New community organizers without an established track record will be an unknown quantity. Even those with well-known brand names may find it difficult to transfer that brand image to an on-line environment and a virtual community setting. Once members have come to rely on virtual communities to address their needs, and they have developed confidence that the community understands them and respects their privacy, they will find it difficult to make a switch.

Other factors are also likely to play a role in the building of switching barriers. At one level, simply becoming familiar with the distinctive "look and feel" of a specific community is likely to make some members loath to change. As communities develop the ability to tailor their offerings to individual members, this will also generate a switching barrier. A new community that lacks a visitor's usage profile will be unable to tailor its offering (for example, displaying a certain sequence of screens based on observing how the person has navigated through the community in the past) even though the technology may be available to all organizers. Agent technology introduces another potential switching barrier: agents typically must learn member preference over time; once members invest significant time and effort, they will think twice about moving to a new community and confronting a new set of agents with no insight into their preferences. There is no substitute for experience.

For all these reasons, churn rates in virtual communities are likely to come down over time. The member loyalty loop outlined above will work to create stronger and stronger ties to a particular community as time passes. The longer a new entrant waits, the more difficult (and expensive) it will be to pry members out of existing communities.

Factor costs increase. Some of the key talent required to build virtual communities today may become much more expensive as time passes.

The most notable examples are the hosts of bulletin boards and chat areas who help to make these vibrant and focused forums for communication. We will have more to say about this skill in chapter 7. Today it is not a highly developed skill, and, where available, it tends to be supplied by individuals who are passionate about on-line communication and are willing to contribute their time for free or for nominal amounts (such as free on-line access). Over time, we anticipate that this skill will become much more highly valued and that talent will command a substantial premium, much as it does in the music or movie industry. Those who enter the virtual community business late will find much of the available talent in this area already preempted by existing community organizers and will have to pay much more to lure it away to a new community devoid of members.

Marketing and data analysis skills will also be essential to the success of communities, and, once again, people having these skills and demonstrating a proven track record in an on-line environment are likely to command a substantial premium. Chapter 7 will also address these skills in more detail.

The result of these emerging markets for scarce skills will be to bid up the price of these factor costs, which represent a substantial portion of operating costs in the early years. What today is available practically free from people with good will is likely to become difficult and expensive to access over time. As these factor costs rise, the investment required to enter the business will rise accordingly.

Concentration limits opportunities for entry. Increasing returns businesses tend toward concentration over time. The next chapter will develop this theme in more detail. For the moment, think about the operating software business—Microsoft and Novell. Think about small package delivery networks—Federal Express and UPS. Think about the credit card business—Visa, MasterCard, and American Express. These are all driven by substantial increasing returns dynamics, and they are all highly concentrated businesses.

The big get bigger— and more profitable.

This tendency is not surprising given the reinforcing effect of dynamic loops in operation. These loops operate over time both to accelerate revenue growth (the big get bigger) and to drive down unit costs (the big get richer). Smaller players have little choice but to redouble their efforts to get bigger or risk getting swallowed by one of the larger players or being shoved into bankruptcy court.

The implication is that those who wait a few years to enter this business are likely to find themselves up against large players in any specific community category. The fragmented atmosphere that now characterizes the on-line world is likely to prevail only in the near term as players jockey for position. The large players to come will enjoy significant scale and scope advantages. As indicated above, major elements of their cost structure will benefit from increasing return dynamics. For example, a large community is likely to experience significantly lower acquisition costs per new member than a new entrant. These scale-related cost advantages are likely to be substantial and pervasive.

Economies of scope will also play a role. As is explained in more detail in chapter 7, community organizers will be able to share specific functions across an entire community covering very broad and diverse areas. In the travel community cited above, for instance, the member support function can be shared across the entire travel community, creating a substantial advantage relative to an emerging community seeking to target a narrower segment of the travel market, like the Hawaii travel community.

The net result is that new entrants will confront a concentrated business driven by large community organizers who enjoy substantial operating cost advantages, clear differentiation through unique assets, and high switching barriers for their existing members. New entrants will therefore have to spend a lot more money than their predecessors did, yet even with bigger stakes on the table, they may not be able to catch up and their investment may be lost. Those who wait will need deep pockets and a high tolerance for risk.

Acquisition becomes very expensive

The other option for those who choose to wait is to buy their way in by acquiring one of the early entrants that has started to ride the revenue acceleration curve. This will be a very expensive option.

Acquisition premiums for network-related businesses are already far above the stock prices for these businesses, which already reflect high multiples (and often infinite, given the lack of any earnings at all). This option is not for the fainthearted. Even allowing for current hype, there is an underlying rationale for high multiples, especially once the revenue acceleration process kicks in. At this point, increasing returns dynamics are in full swing and the prospect of high growth combined with increasing profitability are enough to make any investor take notice. And that is the point. These virtual community initiatives are unlikely to be "hidden" investment opportunities, unnoticed by the broader market. Under the glare of public attention, the value of these initiatives is likely to be fully—perhaps too fully—reflected in stock prices.

As time passes, there is likely to be an additional premium embedded in the acquisition price of a virtual community. This is the value of the virtual community to some of the traditional businesses likely to be threatened by the growth of these new entities. These traditional businesses will probably be willing to pay substantial premiums for the chance to own and control a virtual community once the commercial and competitive potential of the business has become apparent. Since these businesses are likely to realize some synergy values from acquiring a related virtual community (say, an airline acquiring a travel community), they will presumably be willing to pay more than an acquirer from an unrelated business.

This chapter has focused on the economic potential of the virtual community business. Increasing returns dynamics will help to make virtual communities powerful engines of long-term value creation for the astute and aggressive organizer—engines driven by a combination of accelerating revenue growth and declining unit costs. The challenge will be to weather the near-term profit pressures while at the same time pursuing an aggressive growth strategy. Those who aggregate a critical mass of members in any given community topic area will be hard to stop. Later entrants will find an increasingly unwelcome economic environment that will make their entry both expensive and risky.

4

the shape of things to come

Virtual communities are a moving target. Organizers who enter with one view of industry structure may find themselves surprised as the virtual ground beneath them shifts in unanticipated ways. Those who keep their eyes (and investments) focused on member acquisition, information capture, and emerging growth opportunities are likely to profit the most from these changes.

IF YOU ARE GOING TO ESTABLISH A VIRTUAL community—and if you want it to grow and sustain profitability—you need a good understanding of how the industry is likely to evolve. By "industry" we mean the structure of the community business (for example, are there many fragmented communities or a few large ones?) and the relationships that evolve between communities themselves on the network (are they completely independent, or do they develop "trading" and/or ownership ties? if so, are these relationships between equals or between large and small communities?). Growth potential may in fact be quite limited if virtual communities remain highly fragmented niche businesses. Similarly, profitability may be unexpectedly squeezed if virtual community organizers become dependent on other players for member acquisition or end up having to share ownership of members' usage and transaction profiles.

In this chapter we'll describe one likely path of industry evolution and the corresponding stages of development we expect for virtual communities. We will focus on the key assumptions that define each of these four stages while also specifying the contrary assumptions that, if true, might lead the evolution to stall at that stage. These development stages and their underlying assumptions are summarized in the table that follows.

Stage of Evolution	Description	Key Assumptions
Virtual villages	Communities are highly fragmented but profitable businesses, each containing multiple, small subcommunities	• Low barriers to entry • Many entrants • Vendors participate across multiple communities • Network users sample across multiple communities
Concentrated constellations	Concentration of core communities, and development of affiliate relationships with niche communities	• Increasing returns lead to concentration within "core" topics, such as travel • Niche communities benefit from affiliating with core communities
Cosmic coalitions	Core communities aggregate across complementary core topic areas	• Members find value in formation of coalitions, around common user interface and billing, for instance • Coalition organizers realize economic value by integrating marketing programs and member/vendor profiles across topic areas
Integrated infomediaries	Communities and coalitions evolve into agents for members, managing their integrated profiles to maximize value to members	• Members themselves represent the most efficient location for capture of profiles • Members assert ownership over their profiles • Specialized infomediaries can organize and maximize value of member profiles

We believe that virtual communities will evolve from a highly fragmented group of businesses to a much more concentrated industry. This will of course mean that value creation potential will also evolve over time. In the early stages of community evolution, value creation and capture shifts from advertisers and vendors—where much of the value has resided prior to the advent of virtual communities—to the level of the community organizer. At this level, the potential for value capture will be highest for organizers of "core" communities who mobilize and lock in broader constellations of more specialized communities. At the next stage of evolution, value capture will migrate to the organizers of still broader coalitions of complementary communities. These coalitions will be well able to meet member needs.

From chaos to organization— the inevitable path toward concentration.

Finally, long-term winners will begin to emerge from those communities that have evolved from providing members with services to providing them with tools—tools that enable members to maximize the value of their profiles and vendors' profiles in accessing and purchasing resources available on the network. In this way, virtual communities will ultimately shift from packaging network resources to packaging member and vendor profiles. They will act explicitly as agents of their members by helping them maximize their own value as customers.

Reality will certainly be much less clear than the sequential path outlined in this chapter. We can already see elements of later stages of development emerging today on the network. For example, Web sites like Amazon.com are already developing "affiliate" programs that begin to create the "constellations" discussed below. Similarly, America Online represents a likely contender for the role of "coalition organizer" described in a later stage, building position even before many of its constituent communities have emerged.

STAGES OF COMMUNITY EVOLUTION

Our perspective in this chapter on the likely evolution of the virtual community business underscores two key components of value creation in virtual communities: you must focus on information capture and you must exploit growth options aggressively. Community organizers who remain focused on these two imperatives are likely to expand their business scope (for example, from organizing an individual community to organizing a constellation of communities and eventually to organizing a broader coalition of communities) and, in the process, create substantial value.

Virtual villages

In this early stage of development, virtual communities remain small (though still containing up to a few thousand members participating in a variety of small subcommunities) and highly fragmented—virtual villages—with people using search engines to identify those of greatest interest to them. Because there are so many of these communities targeting such a broad range of needs, most individuals are likely to belong to a large number of communities and to spend relatively little time in any one.

At this stage, the winners in terms of value creation and capture are likely to be vendors. Vendors, especially those with strong brand images, will be in a strong negotiating position relative to fragmented community organizers struggling to attract and retain a critical mass of members.

Key assumptions shaping this development stage. The idea that fragmentation defines this stage of development hinges on a number of key assumptions. First, it assumes there will be relatively low barriers to entry for organizers of virtual communities, at least early on. As shown in chapter 3, the capital investment required to establish a virtual community today is relatively low, especially relative to its value and growth potential.

Second, it assumes that many players will see the economic potential and choose to enter the business. Third, it assumes that most major vendors will attempt to place their resources in multiple, competing communities. Vendors are likely to want to maximize their access to audience or customer segments and to avoid the risk of locking into an exclusive relationship with a single community that may or may not succeed. If this is the case, the opportunities for differentiation between virtual communities at the outset are likely to be limited, increasing the potential for fragmentation.

Finally, the expectation of fragmentation assumes that since early virtual communities are likely to have limited resources and even more limited potential for clear differentiation, network users will at the outset choose to browse among a variety of competing communities rather than quickly settling down as members of one community in a given topic area.

Key assumptions that would stall development to the next stage. For evolution to stall at this stage, the increasing returns dynamics described earlier in this book would have to be overwhelmed by some countervailing force. For example, it may be difficult to scale up a meaningful community experience beyond a few thousand members. Much of the value of participating in these virtual communities is presumed to be the trust-based relationships that evolve between members and the corresponding willingness of members to contribute to the accumulation of information residing in the community. As communities grow larger, these trust-based relationships may erode as members find it harder and harder to maintain a sense of intimacy. Instead, confronted with hordes of "newbies" each time they log on, more seasoned members may lose the incentive to contribute their experiences and may spend more time on the sidelines, waiting for others to contribute. As these personal ties erode, seasoned members may find it more tempting to escape from the larger communities and join smaller, more personal ones until growth once again repeats the cycle of alienation and dispersion. As we will see in chapter 7, the development of "tiered" communities could help to address this problem.

A second countervailing force may be the economic incentives for successful talented staff members to "hive" off existing communities and build their own. This phenomenon might be analogous to that seen in professional services firms and creative media ventures, where successful producers discover they can earn more by leaving and starting up companies of their own. Organizers of the first wave of virtual communities will have to create compensation structures that keep their key talent well rewarded. Otherwise, that talent, after demonstrating success in drawing membership, may well leave to capture more value elsewhere. Repeated defections will keep virtual communities from growing beyond a certain size. Chapter 7, which deals with community organization, suggests some actions that can be taken to counteract this tendency toward fragmentation.

A third countervailing force may result from the efforts of vendors to protect their interests. Virtual communities have significant potential to undermine the market power of major vendors. They create an environment in which customers can be aggregated by a third party, provided with information that helps them to choose more effectively between competing vendors, and offered the means to switch easily from one vendor to another. The major vendors are thus likely to look for ways to manipulate the virtual community business model so it works to their own ends.

One option would be for individual vendors to organize "captive" communities. These communities would provide many of the services and capabilities associated with virtual communities, but they would keep competing vendors out. For example, Caterpillar might seek to organize a business-to-business community for construction contractors but exclude other manufacturers of construction equipment from participating. At the same time, Caterpillar might refuse to participate in any independently sponsored community for construction contractors. If Caterpillar's vendor-specific community for construction contractors proves successful, other vendors of construction equipment might seek to organize their own virtual communities, leading to even further fragmentation.

In an effort to weaken virtual communities, vendors could also seek to encourage the formation of competing communities. They might accomplish this by actively subsidizing new communities in markets where one or more communities appear to be gaining disproportionate share or by selectively distributing products across multiple communities to increase the potential for differentiation.

We suspect that efforts by vendors to co-opt, capture, or fragment virtual communities will founder when they encounter two more powerful forces. First and foremost, community members are unlikely to allow this to happen. A key driving force behind community development is likely to be members' growing awareness of the potential power of this new business model to serve their needs and increase their power relative to vendors. What is likely to be the reaction of community members to vendors who seek to restrict their access to competing vendors? Most probably, they will shift their loyalty to community organizers

> *Vendors can try to co-opt, capture, or fragment virtual communities, but their efforts will be in vain.*

who understand their desire for choice—and to the vendors that support them. Furthermore, the increasing returns dynamics described in chapter 3, on value creation, are likely to frustrate efforts by vendors to keep virtual communities fragmented. The subsidies required to counteract the force of these dynamics are likely to be massive.

Fragmentation of virtual communities might also be accomplished by regulatory policies. One indirect way to dampen the increasing returns drivers that push toward concentration would be to restrict freedom to capture information on community members. Usage and transaction information capture is likely to be a major engine for economic growth, providing an incentive for concentration so that ever broader profiles of member transaction activities can be captured. By cutting out this asset, regulators would decrease the value of concentration. More directly, regulators might choose to deploy some variant of antitrust or restraint of trade doctrine to maintain direct control over the size or behavior of virtual community organizers. This is perhaps the most significant countervailing trend. Its likelihood will be strongly influenced by the degree to which community organizers are able to build trust-based relationships with members. As we have already suggested, this trust is a prerequisite for virtual communities' realization of their full commercial potential. If it is built and preserved, regulators are unlikely to feel any need to intervene.

Implications for value capture. If virtual communities are highly fragmented, the implications for value capture are clear. Like the specialty magazine and information services businesses, these enterprises are likely to become profitable niche businesses, limited in size, but generating attractive returns for the organizer. Assuming they are able to get to at least sufficient scale to generate an audience and customer base interesting to advertisers and product or service vendors, virtual communities will be able to tap into advertising and transaction revenues. Member-generated content and relationships between community members become unique assets differentiating communities and providing the basis for sustainable profitability.

Vendors are likely to find virtual communities useful venues for reaching their audiences or customers, but they will retain substantial negotiating power. Since there are many fragmented community organizers seeking to do business with much larger, well-established vendors, it is reasonable to expect that vendors will be in a good bargaining position to minimize how much they might have to pay in sales commissions and to moderate the kinds of terms and conditions they might have to accept to be represented in the community. They would thus avoid the risk of profit squeeze by concentrated community organizers, especially if they negotiate rights to access the relevant usage and transaction information generated within the community.

Since in this scenario no virtual community would be likely to generate sufficient scale to represent a significant share of a market's overall transactions, any impact on the structure of traditional businesses like banking or consumer goods would probably be gradual. There would still be some possibility of squeezing out traditional intermediaries such as retailers and distributors or wholesalers, but the process would take longer to unfold. Hosting—the operation of a "turnkey" network platform for businesses that lack technology expertise—and specialized technical support services would fare well since they would address a large and fragmented customer base with limited incentive or ability to develop deep technical or operating skills.

Implications for entry strategies. Early fragmentation of the virtual community business increases the need to set realistic expectations regarding early growth and profitability potential. At the same time, community organizers should do everything possible to accelerate the process of aggregating a critical mass of members, thereby unleashing the increasing returns dynamics likely to drive concentration. Community organizers should generally avoid negotiating long-term relationships with vendors at this stage, since their negotiating power is likely to be weak and they run the risk of locking into terms that may eventually prove disadvantageous.

If evolution stalls at this stage, even more emphasis will be placed on leveraged investment, given the cap on growth potential. Urgency of investment would be reduced, since the forces driving fragmentation would likely create a continuing set of opportunities for entry or acquisition. Large-scale vendors of products or services would be much more justified in pursuing a "wait and see" attitude, entering later through acquisition of existing communities if necessary. While the cost of buying a community would be large, given the potential profitability, the acquisition price would not be as high as it might be if the community were projected to grow at a fast pace for some time to come. In addition, the risk of being "locked out" would be much reduced for product and service vendors. The major risk would be the opportunity cost associated with the option to create a vendor-sponsored community to deepen relationships with a target customer base.

Concentrated constellations

In the second major stage of evolution, "core" communities in major topic areas—travel, teen interests, or the legal profession for example—will tend to concentrate, resulting in the emergence of two or three very large "core" communities in each major topic category. Each of these concentrated "core" communities would attract a "constellation" of niche communities (travel in the Amalfi coast of Italy for travel, skateboarding for teenagers, patents for lawyers). See figure 4-1.

Simply organizing a community will not be enough.

While these niche communities would remain nominally independent, they would over time become dependent on the "core" community for traffic generation, aggregation of vendors, and aggregation of information capture. This would lead to tighter and tighter links between the niche communities and specific "core" community affiliates, perhaps even including shared back-office functions like member management, billing, and fulfillment.

In this stage of development, the key winners would be the organizers of the core communities who have aggregated a critical mass of members and begun to mobilize broader constellations of more focused communities. They would have significant bargaining power relative to both vendors participating in their core communities and organizers of niche communities in their constellations. The big losers in this stage of development would probably be traditional intermediaries (retailers, wholesalers, and the like), whose primary value added is in information aggregation, and vendors who lack a strong brand image or access to the member profiles compiled by the core community organizers.

Key assumptions shaping this development stage. This development stage is driven in large part by the increasing returns dynamics described in chapter 3. A key assumption is that these increasing returns are at least to some degree topic specific. For example, the

Figure 4-1 Concentrated Constellations: A Travel Example

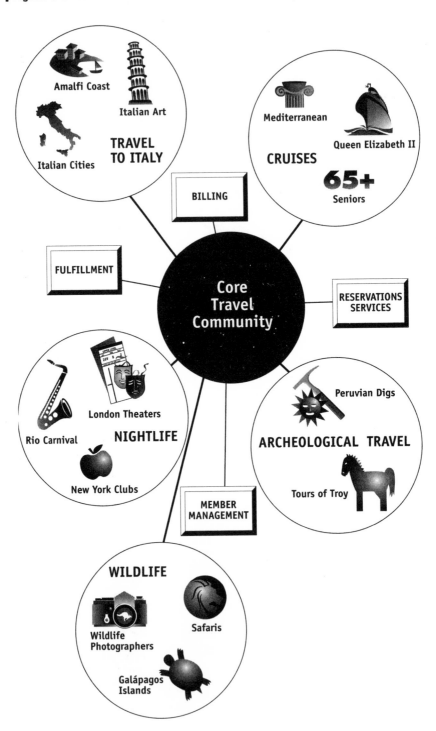

critical mass of members in a travel community would offer little advantage in building a virtual community for health care.

If these increasing returns are topic specific, core communities might, over time, develop subcommunities within the broader topic area. For instance, there is in principle no reason why a well-developed core travel community could not identify and aggregate its members who share a passion and interest in travel to the Amalfi coast. It might then create a distinct set of offerings and environments for these members to enjoy within its broader community offering.

This would work best when there is no existing virtual community targeting those with an interest in travel to the Amalfi coast. What if there is already a thriving community that has targeted this narrow interest and aggregated a significant membership (at least "significant" relative to the degree of interest in the topic)? The larger core community organizer might be able to acquire this community or build out a rival subcommunity of its own.

Either of these options, though, are likely to be quite expensive, given the increasing returns dynamics that the niche community organizer has already unleashed. For the concentrated constellation development stage to play out, it must be too expensive for core communities to acquire or compete directly with niche communities.

How might the organizer of the core community capture much of the value of ownership of the niche community without owning it? One option would be to develop some kind of community "affiliate" program to encourage organizers of niche communities to establish linkages with the core community.

This program could offer affiliates a variety of services, but the most attractive are likely to be traffic generation for the niche community, leveraging the much broader marketing programs of the core community and the aggregation of broader community members. The members of the core community are likely to have at least some interest in the offerings of the niche community and might even become active members of the niche community over time.

The core community might also help its affiliates to offer a broader range of vendors and advertisers to their members. The core community, by virtue of its scale, is likely to have well-established relationships (and some clout) with a large group of travel-related vendors and advertisers. Affiliate communities targeting very narrow travel interests, for example, might still be interested in offering members generic travel services, such as car rental, airline reservations, and travel insurance. The core community could use its broader relationship with these vendors to negotiate tailored offerings on very attractive terms. What kind of terms might a travel insurance provider offer a niche community of 5,000 members? How much better might the terms be if they were negotiated by a core community for 2 million members, representing the combined membership in the core community and its affiliates?

More broadly, the niche community organizers may find affiliation to be the best way to preserve a measure of independence, while at the same time leveraging the benefits of scale. Music producers who create record labels affiliated with much larger record companies and independent film producers who affiliate with major film studios make similar kinds of arrangements, which accommodate the independence that seems most conducive to creativity as well as the economics that tend to favor scale.

In return for these services, the core community might seek to gain access to the vendor and member profiles of the affiliate communities, which would likely be their key asset. An affiliate might readily share these profiles in return for marketing services and information about what its own members do when they spend time in the core community. The core community will be much more effective in developing targeted member acquisition programs for the affiliate communities if it can analyze profiles of their existing members. Similarly, it will be able to negotiate better deals for affiliates with advertisers and vendors if it can be articulate about their member profiles.

Core communities might also benefit by offering a broader range of resources to their own members. By integrating the offerings and member-generated content of affiliates' members into their own directories and search facilities, core communities could create the legitimate impression of a much broader range of offerings and the opportunity to establish a broader network of personal relationships, reducing any incentive members might have to shift to competing communities.

Bulletin board and chat moderators who are passionate about the Amalfi coast and would feel marginalized in a wider-ranging travel community might still be accessible to the core community organizer without being incorporated directly into the core community. This would allow these moderators to maintain some degree of independence and a distinctive identity. In this way, the core community may be able to capture much of the value represented by the niche communities without actually owning them.

Key assumptions that would stall development to the next stage. For evolution to stall at this stage, there would have to be very limited economies of scope across topic areas. From a member perspective, this is most likely to occur if "interest" and topic-related "entertainment" remain the dominant needs served by communities and if little or no value is added to member usage and transaction profiles by extending their scope across constellation types (for instance, "travel" and "health").

If relationship needs are prominently addressed, there is likely to be value to the members in being able to relate to other members not just within the bounds of one constellation but in unrelated types of communities. Similarly, if transaction needs are served, members may find value in the increased buying power that would be made possible by aggregating transaction capability across different constellations. For example, mortgages might be sourced through a personal finance community, a housing and home improvement community, a geographic community, and a young parents community. A constellation organizer interested in aggregating members across all of these communities might be able to obtain far better mortgage terms for them than an individual community organizer.

From the organizer's point of view, a key issue is likely to be the potential value of integrated member usage and transaction profiles across multiple topics. If transactions in single-product or -service categories tend to be concentrated in topic-specific communities, and if advertisers and vendors perceive little value in integrating member profiles across multiple categories, a major economic incentive for aggregation or concentration beyond the topic-specific level would be eliminated.

Implications for value capture. This stage of evolution is perhaps the most favorable to the organizers of virtual communities, in particular the core communities that form the nucleus of a broader constellation of affiliated communities. Not only does the concentration of core communities in specific topic categories create the potential for substantial size and profitability, but the opportunity to develop a broader constellation of affiliates further expands the size and profitability potential of the core community.

Niche community organizers are in a more ambiguous position. On the one hand, they too will benefit from increasing returns dynamics in their more narrowly defined topic areas. After all, how many niche communities on the Amalfi coast are you likely to find over time? Affiliate programs with core communities offer the potential of leverage in marketing and relationships with vendors and advertisers. But affiliate programs also create the potential for an increasing squeeze on profitability as the affiliates become more dependent on core communities for generating key sources of revenue. For example, if the core community ends up generating 85 percent of the new members of an affiliate, the core community might start charging a hefty bounty for each new member generated. The challenge for the affiliates will be to build and maintain sufficiently distinctive assets (most important, an active and loyal membership) to strengthen their negotiating position with core communities.

Product and service vendors may have somewhat uneven prospects for value creation in this stage of evolution. On the one hand, large and concentrated virtual communities represent powerful vehicles for reaching and targeting customers. On the other hand, the concentration among core communities and the increasing dependence of niche communities on the core communities create an unattractive bargaining position for vendors. In particular, the growing scale of the core communities may make it easier for the organizers of these communities to negotiate higher transaction commissions for purchases made by members within the community. The fortunes of these vendors are likely to hinge on their ability to build and maintain a strong brand image relative to the virtual communities and on their ability at least to share in the ownership of information on community member transactions.

Retailers and other kinds of traditional intermediaries may be the most threatened in this stage of evolution. Concentration of virtual communities creates at least the potential for them to disintermediate these traditional players and establish a direct relationship with product and service vendors. Once they have aggregated a critical mass of transactions in a relevant market, virtual communities could seek to capture some of the intermediary margin by challenging the continued value added of these intermediaries. For example, distributors and retailers of entertainment software products might find that a virtual community targeting video game players has achieved sufficient scale to deal directly with software publishers and provide these publishers with an opportunity to sell directly to the members of the community, for an appropriate commission, of course. The ability of intermediaries to defend against this challenge is likely to depend on operational skills in such areas as logistics and fulfillment, as well as scale relative to virtual communities. Highly concentrated intermediaries are likely to fare better than highly fragmented ones.

Implications for entry strategies. Given significant concentration potential driven by increasing returns dynamics, this stage of evolution highlights the need for early entry and aggressive investment to build a critical mass of community members. Selection of an appropriate community focus becomes an important issue in light of the advantaged position of core communities relative to niche communities.

Product and service vendors (as well as traditional intermediaries) would be well advised to evaluate the merits of leading in the organization of relevant virtual communities, given the risk of a profitability squeeze if concentrated communities should emerge between them and their customers. "Waiting and seeing" is likely to be a highly risky strategy under this scenario, given both the rising cost of replicating the capabilities of more mature communities and the rising multiples likely to be required for acquisition of a rapidly growing, well-established community. At best, this could prove a very expensive option. At worst, it could expose vendors to an increasingly unattractive bargaining position relative to the communities that have succeeded in aggregating their target customers.

Cosmic coalitions

In the third stage of development, core communities are aggregated across topic areas by coalition organizers (on-line services like America Online or their equivalent on the Internet). For example, a consumer-focused coalition might aggregate geographic virtual communities to leverage national scale and services while coupling them with a strong local identity and service component. Alternatively, as illustrated in figure 4-2, a consumer coalition might incorporate a broad array of constellations that focus on interests such as travel, personal finance, home ownership, sports, and music. In addition to offering the services shared by the communities within a constellation (such as a reservation system within a travel constellation), a coalition might allow certain functions, such as member acquisition and profile development, to be shared by all constellations within the coalition.

In another example, a coalition might emerge among business-oriented virtual communities that target specific vertical markets, like steel companies, petrochemical companies, and specialty chemical companies. Each individual virtual community would provide deep vertical market focus and expertise, but its participation in a broader coalition would make it easier to deliver to members a set of "horizontal" business services (human resources management, government relations, and so on). These vertical markets all represent process-manufacturing businesses that tend to have certain needs in common. Horizontal services might be tailored to these needs; human resources management could focus on issues involved in skill development of plant staff, for example, while a government relations forum might

Figure 4-2 Cosmic Coalitions: A Consumer Example

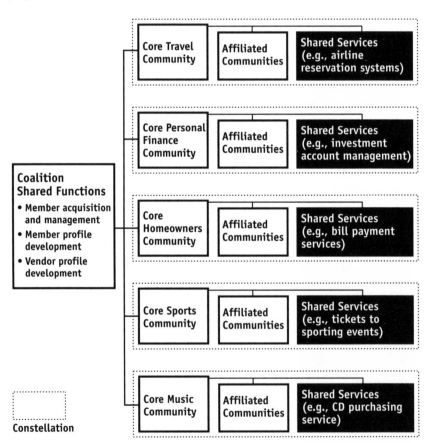

provide news on pending legislation affecting process-manufacturing businesses.

At this stage of development, the winners are those able to organize the broadest coalitions of virtual communities, thereby capturing the primary customer relationships and establishing ownership of member profiles that cut across individual communities. Community organizers, vendors, and traditional intermediaries are vulnerable to the extent that another party with signifi-

> *The best coalitions will think of their members holistically.*

cant negotiating power comes between them and their customers.

Key assumptions shaping this development stage. For this development stage to emerge, compelling value must be created for either the community members or the coalition organizers by integrating ownership across core communities. The value for community members might have several sources: comfort with common user interfaces (for example, the procedures used to locate available resources or the commands used to execute a transaction); assurance of uniform quality across multiple communities coming from development of an overarching brand image and a set of principles governing communication between members; convenience of integrated billing and fulfillment operations across multiple communities; or trust in an overarching coalition organizer to manage the member's usage and transaction profile more effectively across multiple communities.

From the perspective of a coalition organizer, the value of integrating across core communities is likely to reside in two areas: integration of member usage and transaction profiles and leveraging of spending on member acquisition programs. By integrating member usage and transaction profiles across core communities, coalition organizers may be in a position to build a much richer profile of members than any individual community organizer could possess.

A key assumption driving this development stage is that these more integrated profiles would have much greater value to advertisers and product and service vendors than the relatively more fragmented profiles at the community level. For example, they might present a much better indication of intent to purchase. A member of a personal finance community seeking to find a mortgage may be about to purchase a range of services offered in a home owner's and home care community. Even within a single transaction category, people might split their transactions across multiple communities. An avid scuba diver might book flights for diving trips in a scuba diving community, while booking flights for other vacations in a travel community.

In a corresponding way, there may be value in aggregating vendor profiles across communities for the benefit of members. Members might find it helpful to know that the price quoted by a vendor for a specific product or service offered for sale in the community is the best price available from that vendor across a number of communities. Communities might also offer feedback forums for members to post reactions—both positive and negative—to vendor products and services. By aggregating these feedback forums across complementary communities, the coalition organizer might be able to deliver more significant feedback to the members of any one community.

Another assumption is that these profiles could not be aggregated easily or cost effectively by independent information integrators across communities. This assumption hinges on the amount of usage and transaction information "liquidity." Are community organizers able and willing to make their usage and transaction profiles available to third parties to be integrated with profiles from other communities? If not, and if this integrated information has high value, there would be a significant economic incentive for coalition organizers to emerge to accomplish this information integration within a single coalition of "owned" communities.

Another incentive driving coalition formation could be the opportunity to leverage member acquisition expenditures. We have already seen that this is likely to be the single most important expense category in community formation. It may be possible to leverage this expenditure across multiple, complementary communities, drawing members into the coalition and then merchandising the services of the complementary communities forming part of the coalition. This in turn could give independent community organizers a significant advantage. Assuming there is value to either members or coalition organizers in the formation of coalitions, it is possible that these coalitions might evolve naturally (through a process of "fractal" community growth, described in the next chapter) rather than through acquisition of existing communities.

Key assumptions that would stall development to the next stage.
Clearly, one of the most powerful assets accumulated by coalition organizers is the set of integrated profiles of coalition members and vendors. As long as they retain ownership of this asset and the continued
authority to add to it over time, coalition organizers remain in a significantly advantaged position. If they maintain this position, the evolution of virtual communities could stall at this stage of development.

Evolution might also stall at this stage of development if the technologies used by communities to organize and present resources maintain their lead over user-driven technologies that help members to
locate and access resources on the broader network. For example, could
someone use a general purpose directory like Yahoo! or a particular
agent technology to locate quickly and conveniently all the information
she might need on the latest developments in medical imaging technology? Or could a community organizer do a better job of sifting
through, organizing, and presenting this information in a community
targeting health care professionals? If the technologies used by communities maintain an edge over the technologies available to network
users, users would continue to rely on specialized businesses to aggregate and organize the resources they need on the network. Virtual communities or coalitions of communities would remain service businesses
with "locked in" members.

Implications for value capture. At this stage, value capture would probably shift from the community and constellation organizers to the coalition organizer. For example, by having unique access to aggregated
usage and transaction profiles, coalition organizers could extract a larger
cut on advertising and transaction revenues relative to community
organizers. Further, with marketing focused largely at the coalition
level, the primary customer relationship is likely to remain at the coalition level rather than the community level. In much the same way that
a member joins America Online and not one of AOL's individual communities, a member would join a coalition rather than an individual
community. This would give the coalition organizer more leverage in
shaping member usage and transaction patterns through how it chooses
to merchandise different parts of the coalition.

As in the concentrated constellation development stage above, this
stage represents a mixed blessing for product and service vendors. The

much richer usage and transaction profiles will help vendors target potential buyers more effectively, but this benefit must be balanced against the greater negotiating power of coalition organizers in charging for access to these profiles. Imagine a vendor of business telephone equipment being able to analyze telephone equipment purchases (all related purchases, not just this vendor's products) over time, by specific company, to spot high-growth customers. Then imagine this vendor being able to anticipate new equipment purchase decisions by these growth customers by studying their acquisition of new office space. Consider what a coalition organizer might be able to charge for access to such a broad and unique range of information. Once again, the primary defense of product and service vendors is to build strong brand identities based on outstanding product value and to share in the ownership of usage and transaction profiles of the coalitions.

Traditional intermediaries like retailers and wholesalers are even more threatened in this stage of development. Large-scale coalition organizers will be able to generate higher volumes of transactions than core community organizers and will be well positioned to build direct relationships with product and service vendors. Traditional intermediaries are likely to be increasingly squeezed in terms of margins and run the risk of being squeezed out altogether, unless they can leverage operational skills and scale in logistics and fulfillment to carve out a sustainable value-added role.

Implications for entry strategies. This third stage of development heightens the urgency core community organizers should feel to focus on accelerated and aggressive entry strategies. Now, however, they must also focus on the likely dynamics and consequences of coalition formation. The ideal entry strategy would be to focus on the formation of a core community that can provide a growth platform for natural evolution into a coalition of complementary communities over time. If coalition organizers are likely to capture increasing value over time, the aggressive community organizer will want to evolve naturally but quickly into being a coalition organizer, ideally without having to embark on an expensive acquisition program to fill out the coalition portfolio of communities.

One option would be for a community organizer to develop laterally (a process in which related communities would be added through "fractal" growth, which is explained in the next chapter). Another option available to community organizers would be to form a coalition among complementary communities themselves. The goal would be to create some form of cooperative that would pool usage and transaction profiles, undertake joint marketing initiatives, and deliver some of the values that users might look for in a relationship with a coalition as opposed to a community (integrated billing and common ways of indexing materials, for instance). By creating a cooperative, these community organizers might be able to enjoy the benefits of participation in a coalition without the corresponding risk of a profit squeeze by a coalition owner/organizer.

From the viewpoint of an aspiring coalition organizer, entry strategies will need to be just as aggressive, if not more aggressive, than they are for community organizers. Waiting for communities to emerge and concentrate before organizing a coalition is likely to be expensive and difficult. As we have seen, buying rapidly growing communities is likely to be very expensive. Convincing them to join a coalition organized by a third party is likely to be difficult, at least if the coalition organizer aspires to capture a significant portion of the value created over time.

A far better approach for the coalition organizer would be to enter the market quickly, acquire members aggressively, and present a valuable set of services that would persuade community organizers to build their communities in the network environment created by the coalition organizer. America Online represents a non-Internet-based player that has astutely positioned itself as a powerful coalition organizer. It has invested heavily in preemptive member acquisition and created a rich development and operational environment for community organizers (as exemplified by Rainman, America Online's development tool kit), becoming one of the most active seedbeds for community formation.

On the Internet itself, the role of coalition organizer might be played by a number of participants, including Internet service providers, directory service providers, and billing and payment services. Each of these categories of player has the potential to rapidly aggregate traffic that might be directed toward affiliated communities, to build integrated usage and transaction profiles of this traffic, and to deliver value-added services to community organizers. Another type of player that might aspire to the role of coalition organizer is the hosting service, which provides a turnkey development and operating environment for community organizers, including the facilities for capturing and storing usage and transaction profiles. It would be a natural extension for this host to offer to integrate these usage and transaction profiles across affiliated communities.

In all these cases, the challenge for the aspiring coalition organizer will be to negotiate ownership—or at least management—rights to the usage and transaction profiles accumulated by the affiliated communities. These usage and transaction profiles provide the coalition organizer with the ability to become a more effective channel for advertising and transaction revenue, as well as providing insights that will be helpful in targeting membership acquisition programs at the coalition level. In many respects, the balance of ownership rights to usage and transaction profiles between coalition organizer and community organizer will shape the balance of value creation opportunity between the two.

Integrated infomediaries

In this fourth stage of development, virtual communities (or coalitions) evolve into specialized and trusted intermediaries that help members capture integrated profiles of their own activities on-line and then manage this information on their behalf.

Previous evolutionary stages all began with the assumption that the key challenge for the community organizer and participating vendors is to capture more detailed information about a broad range of members. This stage of development turns that assumption on its head and anticipates

Members may choose to own their information themselves.

that, in the end, members will choose to capture information about themselves so they can maximize the value from that information. If this plays out, community or coalition organizers might be well positioned to play an intermediary role in helping members collect and manage this information. The key difference is that ownership of the information would remain with the member and not with the community or coalition organizer.

Many of the roles that such an infomediary would play are quite consistent with—and are in fact natural extensions of—the community services discussed earlier in this book. An infomediary could use the member's usage and transaction data to filter incoming advertisements. An infomediary could also serve as an agent, searching the network for information likely to be useful to the member given specific usage and transaction patterns. For example, if a member has just purchased a home in a new area, the infomediary, based on knowledge that the member belonged to a health club near his previous home, would begin collecting information about local health clubs. An infomediary could also help the member organize usage and transaction data for such applications as budgeting, tax planning, and estate planning. The infomediary might provide selected vendors with limited access to member information to help them more effectively tailor their products and services to the member's needs. Finally, the infomediary would help the member maximize the economic value of this information by auctioning the rights of controlled access to it, consistent with the privacy preferences of the member.

To the extent that community or coalition organizers evolve into this role, their focus may expand beyond organizing a distinctive content and communication environment for members to managing the information asset (which could extend well beyond the profile of activities in a single community or coalition to encompass the full range of on-line—and perhaps even off-line—activities of the member). In fact, to do this effectively and credibly, the community or coalition organizers may ultimately have to spin off their initial community or coalition offerings to avoid the appearance of bias in favoring their community or coalition. In this way, the virtual community business might evolve into one based purely on information management for members.

In fact, if user-driven aggregation tools evolve rapidly enough, it is possible that the community business could evolve increasingly from a service business to a tool business. In other words, the primary source of value added could become the development and sale of software tools that help users to aggregate resources on their own and to maximize the value of their own usage and transaction information capture.

The winners in this development stage will be those coalition and community organizers that successfully evolve into infomediaries. Anyone who has built a business model assuming exclusive and permanent ownership of key customer information will be vulnerable. More generally, those who lack the skills to extract maximum value from information about customers will also be vulnerable since they will be unsuited to the role of infomediary. They will also find themselves increasingly shut out from access to key customer information because they are unable to deliver enough value in return for access to it.

Key assumptions shaping this development stage. This stage of development hinges on three key assumptions. The first is that the PC can become an efficient and convenient device for the capture of a truly comprehensive usage and transaction profile of anyone accessing a network like the Internet (that is, a network user). Technology already embedded in popular Internet browsers indicates that users of the network can transparently capture very detailed profiles of the full range of their own on-line activities with software installed on their PC. The so-called cookie technology originally introduced by Netscape as a feature of its browser captures information about the specific activities of the user on individual Web sites and stores this information in the user's PC.

The second assumption is that privacy issues will make it increasingly difficult for vendors (or community or coalition organizers) to capture as detailed and comprehensive a set of information as users themselves can on their PCs. The paradox is that the better the technology becomes at capturing information, the more concern people will have about their privacy. The only way to resolve this paradox may be to acknowledge that users themselves are the rightful owners of their own usage and transaction information. Once this leap is made, users can be equipped with robust information capture capability and allowed to determine whether, and on what terms, to make usage and transaction information available to third parties. Privacy disappears as an issue because information disclosure is at the discretion of the user.

The third assumption is that users will seek the services of specialized and trusted intermediaries—infomediaries—to take on the task of organizing this information and maximizing the value that can be derived from it. As seen above, the value to the user can take many forms, and in most cases the bulk of the value is likely to be in the form of nonmonetary convenience and access to more tailored products and services.

Over time, it may be possible for users themselves to perform the many roles of the infomediary with a powerful set of technology tools consisting of intelligent filters, agents, expert systems, and auction software. For the foreseeable future, however, the assumption is that there will be a valuable role for a physical, and human, agent to help users collect and manage the usage and transaction data. This is especially true if infomediaries also aggregate vendor profiles for members and add value by developing ways to cross-match this information with member profiles. For example, based on an understanding of the situations in which a vendor of office equipment is most likely to discount prices, a community organizer targeting office managers might work with members to structure their purchases in ways that would increase the probability and amount of discount.

If these specialized infomediaries arise, it is likely that community or coalition organizers will be natural candidates for the role. They will have developed a trusting relationship with their members, based on the reputation for quality and reliability that is likely to accrue to successful communities. More important, the communities and coalitions will be positioned as champions of member interests in their dealings with the broad range of product or service vendors relevant to the community. In addition, the community and coalition organizers will have deep expertise in the technology and management issues surrounding both the capture of on-line information and its application to the generation of economic value.

Implications for value capture. At this stage of their development, virtual communities are unlikely to own one of the key assets driving value creation in the earlier stages of development—detailed usage and transaction profiles of members. These will be owned neither by the virtual community nor even by the coalition but by members themselves. In this situation, long-term value capture by virtual communities and coalitions will depend on their ability to transform themselves into trusted custodians of this information and to charge appropriate fees for services rendered. Communities and coalitions that do not make this transition may find that their investments in community building and related usage and transaction information capture fail to make an adequate return.

To the extent that community coalitions emerge, the owners of these coalitions may be advantaged relative to individual community organizers. Coalition organizers may be in a better position to make the transition to specialized infomediary because of the breadth of their relationship with members and the deeper experience they develop in managing a broader range of member information.

Value creation for product and service vendors at this stage of development will depend on their ability to execute a similar shift in focus. The potential for above-average returns in this development stage will depend less on privileged access to customer information and much more on the skills required to take that information and deliver tangible value back to the customer, while at the same time maximizing the commercial value for the vendor. These skills include the ability to focus on categories of customer information that have the greatest commercial potential, to identify the specific commercial opportunities residing in the customer information, and to address these commercial opportunities quickly. Product and service vendors who have greater skills in this area will be in the best position to make the highest bid for the rights to access this information from the usage and transaction profiles accumulated by network users. In contrast with the situation today, when information is captured as a by-product of interaction with the customer, customers in this new world may deny access to the information unless the vendor is prepared to pay more for it than anyone else.

Once again, traditional intermediaries will be relatively disadvantaged in this development stage. Much of the value creation by retailers and wholesalers over the past several decades has been the result of superior access to customer information. If customers begin to assert ownership over this information and the right to make it broadly available to the highest bidder (or not to make it available at all), this privileged access by retailers and wholesalers will erode. The ability to continue to create value will hinge on value-added services *not* based on this information.

Implications for entry strategies. This evolutionary stage of development emphasizes an even earlier need to develop deep skills in the extraction of commercial value from member usage and transaction profiles. Those community organizers with the greatest skills in this area will be more credible in their efforts to become custodians of this information.

This stage of development also increases the importance of developing an explicit position as the champion of member interests rather than as a representative of the vendors seeking to reach members. Specifically, this means taking aggressive action to help equip members with the tools necessary to maximize their ability to capture value relative to the vendors in the community. By adopting this position, the community organizer will be able to emerge as the trusted custodian of member usage and transaction profiles instead of as a biased agent of vendors seeking to reach the members.

REFLECTING ON POTENTIAL OUTCOMES

This overview of the potential evolution of the virtual community business highlights several themes. First, it suggests that this is an evolving battle with enormous stakes. What is really at issue is who will own the customer, at least on networks and perhaps even more broadly. Second, the best way to "own" the customers may in fact be to champion the customers, providing them with the tools they need to increase their bargaining power relative to vendors. This provides a basis for loyalty and trust that will be deep and long lasting. Third, the focus of many virtual community businesses over time is likely to shift from providing information and communication services for members to providing a transaction environment that fully leverages the power of the members as customers. Fourth, the potential for value creation at any point in time will hinge on a key question: who owns the member usage and transaction profiles accumulated in virtual communities? Finally, virtual communities represent powerful platforms for growth, and organizers who aggressively exploit this potential, addressing an ever broader range of member needs for an ever broader range of members, are likely to be the winners.

"Owners" of the customer will be "champions" of the customer.

II

building
a virtual
community

CHAPTER

5

choosing the way in

Deciding where you *want* to compete in the virtual community business requires some knowledge of where you *can* compete. What types of communities are likely to emerge from the many possibilities? What are their near- and long-term indicators for profitability and growth? What do we know about a company's assets and skills that can inform us of its chances for future on-line success? This chapter provides some of the parameters you can use as you begin the process of selecting where to build a virtual community.

IN THE PRECEDING CHAPTERS WE'VE LAID OUT a case for why the virtual community business is shaping up as a battle with enormous stakes. We've taken a close look at the economics of these communities to give you an idea of how they can lead to real profits. And we've examined the ways in which the virtual community industry as a whole is likely to evolve as it matures.

What we haven't done yet is to discuss the more pragmatic issues of how your company can begin to think about getting into the virtual community business. What are the different entry points? How do you evaluate them? What are the criteria for choosing where to compete in the virtual community industry?

In this chapter, we'll begin answering these questions with an eye toward helping you understand which of your assets and skills you can leverage to take advantage of the potential virtual communities hold. Subsequent chapters will discuss what specific entry strategies you might employ as well as how to organize yourself once you've made that entry and how to think about the technological challenges you're likely to encounter.

There are three levels along which the decision on where to compete must be made. The first two have to do with which types of community (in the consumer and business-to-business worlds) are most likely to create value in the near term and in the long term. The third examines whether some companies are better positioned than others to organize a given community; is there such a thing, in other words, as a "natural owner" in the virtual community industry?

INDICATORS OF NEAR-TERM ECONOMIC POTENTIAL

Most players on the Web have "fallen into" organizing a certain type of site, largely as a result of prior interests or the desire to expand an existing business directly on-line. Fewer players have systematically scanned all the possibilities, segmented the market, and focused on an area because of its economic advantages. This is understandable given that the industry itself is so new. But players must now begin deliberately assessing what type of community they want to organize *before* entering the arena. There are several factors that, with some confidence, we can predict will have an impact on communities' value. As we will explain, some types of community will benefit from these factors more than others, and the pathway into organizing a certain type of community may not be obvious at first glance. Should a bank selling auto loans help organize a community for those interested in cars, for parents with young families, or for suburban homeowners?

> *The pathway into the virtual community business may not be obvious.*

Having gone through the exercise a number of times now, we believe that if you brainstorm long enough, it's possible to justify the existence of a virtual community in any arena you care to mention. But communities do vary in their inherent potential to create value. Several factors drive this potential.

Size of potential community

Estimating the maximum potential size of a given type of community involves triangulating into an answer by assessing several factors.

Demographic statistics can help. For a parenting community, the starting point is the number of parents. If the community has a certain focus, the group may have to be broken down further. You may want to set up a community for Spanish-speaking parents, for example. If you are setting up a community devoted to a city such as London, what might the most relevant measure of the community be? The number of people who live in the city, those who work in the city, the total number of annual visitors, or some combination of all three? It will depend on the focus you are choosing for the community.

Spending information is an even more important indicator of the size of your target group. In the case of travel, the number of people who have spent money on travel in the past twelve months would be one indicator of the community's total potential size. Sometimes—and travel is a case in point—it's important to define the scope of the community carefully: is it a community for all travelers, or is it just for leisure, or business, travelers? Another measure is the number of people buying information about the arena in question. How many people subscribe to magazines or journals? How many people subscribe to electronic information services related to the topic?

Membership in associations or groups is another strong indicator, since activity in these associations often demonstrates a more than casual level of interest in the target area in question. These associations or groups could include industry associations, hobbyist groups, or representative groups such as the American Association for Retired Persons.

These factors all need to be taken into account to arrive at the best estimate of the community's potential size. Given the nature of the medium, it's also important to remember to include people in other geographic areas: English-speaking communities can draw on members from many other countries beyond the United States and the United Kingdom.

Relative value of being on-line

It's one thing for there to be, say, 15 million people potentially interested in travel. But how many of them might end up on-line? This is partly a function of the number of those people who are physically equipped to go on-line. How many of them own or have access to PCs equipped with modems? How easy, or how expensive, is it to connect to the network? Then there is a more subjective set of factors: How much value does the on-line medium add to off-line alternatives? Would an on-line service be cheaper or more efficient in some significant way? Would an on-line service provide unique capabilities, such as the ability to find and connect with individuals or businesses that would otherwise be hard to find?

In the case of sports, communities connect fans in ways that magazines or even sporting events cannot: in a community, fans can swap stories, give each other tips, and compete against each other with mock teams. Other kinds of communities will help customers compare products: home buyers looking for mortgages might more easily compare dozens of alternatives by going on-line than by calling each bank separately and dealing with customer service. Banks might even encourage this so as to avoid paying mortgage brokers' fees. Small export businesses would value the time saved by a community offering them "one-stop shopping" for everything from stationery and office supplies to tariff information and currency hedging services. In markets that are fragmented, or where geography creates barriers, the on-line arena can make a major difference in helping suppliers identify customers and vice versa. Gardeners looking for rare plants can find the nurseries that sell them. Buyers of used, specialized equipment can find those prepared to sell it.

Value of being in a community

We described earlier how communities satisfy our need to interact for purposes of relationship, interest, transaction, and fantasy. That being so, another measure of the potential of a community is the intensity of these needs among its potential members. Parents, for example, are hungry for information on countless aspects of child rearing. They have emotional ups and downs in the process, which many of them are eager to share with other parents. They also need to make a wide array of purchases (such as health care services, strollers, baby foods) that could be made more efficiently and effectively with advice from previous buyers. A parenting community is therefore likely to score highly in terms of the value it would bring to its members. On the business front, communities focused on markets where products are complex and hard to evaluate (such as sophisticated software or precision equipment) might be enormously valuable for members, who would want to compare experiences with other purchasers of the same goods.

Likely intensity of commerce

It can be helpful to understand the volume of transactions conducted by the targeted community group, the average size of each transaction, and the amount of advertising currently spent to reach them. But it can also be tempting to focus too much on this factor; it is, after all, only one of several. As we have said before, community must come before commerce. Still, it's worth understanding this factor early on, especially if it might constrain a community's economic upside later. A community for artists is never likely to match the economic potential of a community for parents, however much work they sell and however rich the community's patrons.

Fractal depth

A community's "fractal depth" is the degree to which it can be segmented. The spirit of community, as reflected in the importance of the relationships between and the roles of community members, is what makes a virtual community such a powerful business model. If this spirit tends to be greater in smaller groups where it's possible for people to have more in common, then the more ways a community can be split into smaller subcommunities the better. We call this a community's "fractal depth."

Let's pick an example to illustrate this concept. A travel community can segment itself along several different lines: by geography, by travel type (air travel, cruises, train journeys), and by reason for travel (culture, history, hobby, sport). Taking the geographic angle for a moment, it can fragment according to continent, within continents by country, and within countries by city. (See figure 5-1.) Over time it can evolve into a rich set of subsegments. It is impossible to predict precisely what will emerge, because it all depends on members' preferences. Perhaps small communities will materialize for denizens of Venice, fans of the Orient Express, or trekkers in the Himalayas. No one can know until the community develops and takes on a life of its own. But it is still possible to analyze what *might* emerge and thereby to assess a community's potential depth.

Use "fractal depth" to create focus and stronger member ties.

Fractal depth can be a helpful indicator of the value the community will have to advertisers and vendors. The more ways a community can be split, the more it can create small, focused subcommunities to which its members will be more dedicated (and in which they'll spend more time) than they would to a community with hundreds of thousands of users. In this sense, complexity is healthy. Additionally, the more focused a subcommunity, the deeper the interests its members are likely to have, and the more open and eager they are likely to be to receive relevant advertisements and engage in transactions.

In chapter 4 we discussed how the virtual community industry might evolve over time. We talked about the potential emergence of "constellations" of communities, in which communities that shared certain characteristics might ally themselves with one another. Organizers of the strongest communities would stand to gain power within these constellations. A measure of who is "strongest" will be the degree to which a community has been able to establish depth in a given area and so position itself to become a "core" community. Fractal depth will therefore enable a community to push toward the next stage of growth.

COMMUNITY TYPES

In assessing the growth potential of different communities using the criteria described, where do you begin? There are countless possibilities.

Figure 5-1 "Fractal" Communities

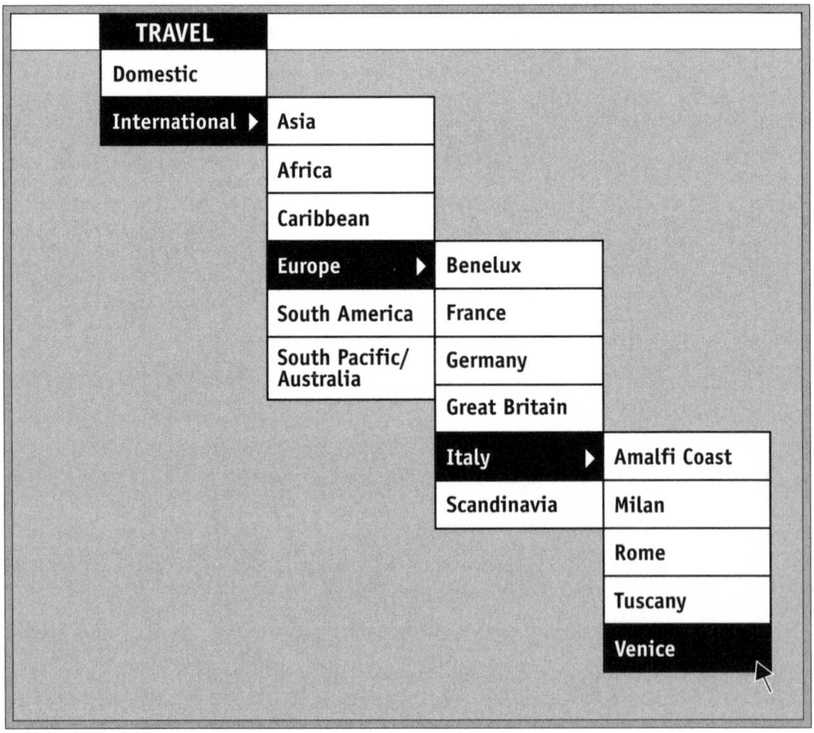

How do you think about them in a way that prevents you from missing an obvious opportunity? It will help to think in terms of the basic kinds of commercial communities likely to evolve over the next few years.

Consumer-focused communities

In a consumer environment, community development may take place in one of three directions: geographic, demographic, or topical. Dividing up the world of potential communities along these lines can help ensure that, at least on a broad level, you don't miss an opportunity.

Geographic communities. Geographic communities are formed around a physical location in which all the community's participants have a common interest—generally because they are physically located there. On-line sites that focus on all parts of the world are already sprouting up. New York, home to many Internet start-ups, has several. One of the better known and developed is Total New York ("where New York hits the Net"), which offers hip editorials on New York culture ("PULSE—the culture beat") and information about what's going on in Manhattan ("URBAN ACCESS—the complete guide to NYC"). It boasts more than 30,000 listings of restaurants, galleries, stores, and more; reviews of art, dance, and theater; forums featuring prominent writers; and chat areas for discussing weekend plans, among other things. Another, Metrobeat, focuses on information about New York events and offers maps to locate them. Sites are springing up in areas as diverse as Amsterdam (the Amsterdam Channel), Russia (Russia Alive!), and South Africa (where the Electronic Mail & Guardian offers news, an employment section to post resumes, and a sports-betting calendar, described as South Africa's first on-line casino).

Members value these sites because of the information they provide about what is going in their physical community. These can also stimulate local political and social interaction. One local American newspaper, the *South Bend Tribune* in Indiana, for example, put a summary of its county budget on-line. Readers could download the budget in spreadsheet form, analyze it, post comments to one another on a bulletin board, and ask questions of the county's assistant auditor in an on-line forum. The results were written up in the paper.

Based on our criteria for what creates value in a virtual community, geographic communities may look especially attractive in the near term if they are focused on large regions or cities that have strong subcommunities within them. But their effectiveness as vehicles for transactions—such as ordering take-out meals or booking tickets—may be relatively limited.

Demographic communities. Demographic communities focus on gender, life stage, or ethnic origin. Examples include communities for teens, single parents, empty-nesters, and seniors. This kind of community is only just beginning to emerge, but initial indicators suggest it can be very attractive to participants. We mentioned ParentsPlace earlier. Parent Soup is another parenting site offering a mix of bulletin boards and chat areas on such "ingredients" as "Baby," "Money," "Sports," "Travel," and "Personals." "Parent to Parent Bulletin Boards" cover topics as wide ranging as adoption, multilingual families, parents of only children, "parents' picks" (which offers goods and services recommended by other parents), and personals: "Single parents—come find a summer companion on-line!" is one example. One of the many ethnic sites is PhoenixTeaHouse. As part of a community for Asian Americans, it gathers articles, letters, and other information on topics that include business ("Tea Trader"), health and fitness, and job opportunities. It also provides bulletin boards and chat forums. The value proposition of all the above-mentioned sites is that they enable people to "find" each other across geographic boundaries. A seniors' community might help individuals find traveling companions for cruises or long journeys, while a children's community might help a youngster with a particular interest—whether it be making model airplanes or dealing with a particular illness—to find other children with the same interest. Demographic communities are likely to score highly on the size criterion, will generally meet deeper generational needs than geographic communities, and, in some cases (such as those for young families, who also tend to be home buyers), will stimulate high-value transactions.

Topical communities. Topical communities center on topics of interest (excluding geography, gender, or life stage) and include communities focused on hobbies and pastimes such as painting, music, or gardening and on issues of interest such as politics or spiritual beliefs. Many sites today are topically focused, and a few of these could be described as emerging communities. In the area of personal investments, we have already mentioned AOL's Motley Fool. Another emerging community in this field is Silicon Investor, a site with more than 48,000 users that offers published content such as company profiles and articles prepared by the site's writers; analytical tools that allow an investor to compare stock performance across companies within a subindustry and then generate charts graphing performance; and a chat forum for discussions about technology stocks. In a good example of communications being integrated with content, comments from registered users of the site are posted alongside the charts of the respective stock's performance.

An emerging travel community is Travelocity, which is owned by AMR, the parent of American Airlines. It offers a guide to events and activities worldwide; articles by travel writers; bulletin boards; chat forums where you can talk to travel writers about traveling with children or pets; and the ability to purchase tickets, luggage, travel guides, and other merchandise. The value of topical communities lies in their ability to give people of similar interests access to each other and to specialized information. Topical communities will tend to vary widely in potential size, but score highly on transactions and fractal depth because of the intensity and dedication they are likely to tap into among members.

Business-to-business communities

There are also likely to be many communities focused on businesses as opposed to consumers. These need to be thought about differently.

Vertical industry communities. The vertical industry community is likely to be one of the more widespread forms of early business community. Perhaps the most numerous emerging examples are in the high-tech industry, especially software, where developers are forming user groups to give and get advice on selecting software tools and to give each other support beyond what the customer service desk of major software companies can provide. In some cases, these user groups are turning around and providing their software supplier with feedback.

There are many other examples of emerging vertical communities, such as Physicians Online, Agriculture Online, Biospace (which serves the biotech industry), and Virtual Garment Center (which serves the apparel industry and carefully focuses on matching suppliers and buyers). These sites provide information and can allow people in the same industry to network with one another efficiently. Many of them are only just beginning to facilitate and encourage interaction between their members. Agriculture Online, for example, offers an agricultural news service, editorial features from *Successful Farming* magazine (published by the organizer of the site), and bulletin boards, which appear to be well used. The most active of these is Farming Weather.

Counsel Connect Web, an on-line service for lawyers, offers bulletin boards on legal news articles, access to Experts On Call, an Internet concierge service that searches out resources on the Internet, a database of lawyers, and classified ads from several law journals around the United States. Such communities are likely to vary in size according to the size of the industry concerned as well as the degree to which they lend themselves to being on-line. The greater the penetration of PC-based technology in a given industry, the more likely it is that communities will emerge and create value.

Functional communities. This type of community will serve the needs of users representing a specific business function, such as marketing or purchasing. Sites range from IBEX (purchasing information) to one sponsored by the Council of Logistics Management. Today the informational and networking needs of functional managers are served primarily by specialized magazines, industry associations, trade shows, and conferences. Virtual communities could add significantly to this set of options. They will facilitate networking for an emerging generation of managers who are comfortable interacting electronically, although their on-line interactions are unlikely to substitute entirely for trade shows and industry conferences. As existing (noncommercial) virtual communities have already demonstrated, people will continue to have a strong need to meet face to face.

Functional communities will also help managers process information more efficiently. Participants will be able to access more information than ever before and to access it selectively. For example, a company called Individual, Inc., can insert each day into a manager's e-mail box a set of news articles on companies that the manager has preselected. The attractiveness of functional communities is likely to depend on the same criteria as that of vertical industry communities—namely, if the function in question is large and relatively literate in on-line technology. Communities are therefore most likely to spring up first among IT, research and development, and market research professionals and to spread from there into marketing and possibly sales, finance, human resources, and operations.

Geographic communities. We discussed geographic communities in the section on consumer-oriented communities, and we believe they are likely to appear in business communities as well. They may be an off-shoot of local consumer communities, in which businesses catering to the needs of the consumers in a specific location feel a need to start communicating with one another. A Cincinnati community might have within it, for example, a Cincinnati business roundtable site or a Rotary Club site. Small-business or franchise proprietors in the area might value a channel that lets them converse about their particular needs and concerns and gives them access to services that might make their businesses more efficient and their lives easier.

Business category communities. The business category community would be geared to meet the needs of certain types of companies, such as small businesses (the World Association of Small Businesses has an on-line site, for example) or franchises. Also falling into this category would be communities of exporters, which today might interact through governmental trade institutions. These groups do not fall into any industry, geographic, or functional area, but they do have a shared set of needs for information and would benefit from regular interaction with other similar businesses. Because such groups tend not to be well served in terms of networking and information—principally because they cannot afford the time and expense—they may make highly attractive virtual communities from a value perspective. If their needs are met, they may be willing to pay community organizers a hefty premium.

INDICATORS OF LONG-TERM EXPANSION

We have talked about "fractal depth" (the degree to which a community can be segmented) as a driver of near-term economic value. Looking longer term, "fractal breadth" is likely to be an important factor in determining a community's prospects for growth and value creation.

The concept of fractal breadth

Fractal breadth consists of the ability to build out to arenas that bear no relation to the community's original focus. Successful expansion by a community organizer into unrelated topic areas might encourage smaller community organizers in the new areas to ally themselves with the strong organizer in order to preempt further entry into their space, especially if they are not far along in understanding how to aggregate members and establish loyalty.

"Fractal breadth" provides the springboard for growth.

If a community lends itself to being built out from its original core, its organizer puts itself in a good position to become a coalition organizer. The paths along which it might extend itself in this way lead to the same community types we have been describing.

Community types as growth vectors

At this point it may be helpful to think of the types of consumer community—geographic, demographic, and topical—as pathways, or vectors, along which organizers can enter the business of organizing communities. Taking this a step further, each vector becomes an axis from which organizers can branch out into areas on a different axis.

A topical community such as travel could develop a subcommunity focused on the travel needs of parents with young children. From there it could branch out into a demographic community aimed at meeting the full range of needs of parents of young children and perhaps, more broadly, of parents as a whole. (See figure 5-2.) The travel community could also develop subcommunities focused on certain destinations such as Venice. Over time, such a subcommunity could grow to include not just travelers to Venice but residents of Venice (perhaps expatriates living there), and so become a geographic community in its own right. From there it could expand to other Italian cities or to other cities with large expatriate communities. Finally, taking a different tack, a travel community—which is itself a topical community—could expand into other topical communities. For example, a travel subcommunity might emerge that is focused on yachting holidays. This could develop into a separate community aimed at yacht owners.

Because we are still so early on in the life cycle of virtual communities, there is as yet no bona fide example of this kind of fractal breadth. But we would expect geographic and demographic communities to branch out from their axes in much the same way as the topical travel community just described. A geographic community focused on Atlanta might begin to generate subcommunities of members who share a passion in such areas of interest as sports or travel. It might also produce subcommunities organized around demographic groups such as teenagers and senior citizens. Conversely, a senior citizen community might spawn geographic subcommunities (say in Atlanta) and interest-driven subcommunities (say around music), as it expands its membership. Once formed, these subcommunities might form the nuclei of broader communities in their own right that extend well beyond the original focus of their sponsoring communities.

On the business side, the same concept is likely to apply. The organizer of a vertical industry community such as apparel could over time see the community branch out into functional communities. Perhaps it would start with garment buyers at retail stores and grow from there into the field of purchasing. Given the large number of family businesses in the apparel industry, the same apparel community might expand into a category community for small businesses. (See figure 5-3.)

Good long-term prospects

Strategically, it is possible that one of these vectors may prove to be an inherently more effective long-term growth vehicle than the others. If so, which one?

If, as we suggested in chapter 4, gathering a critical mass of community members in turn gives a community a greater chance of splitting into subcommunities, then the demographic and geographic

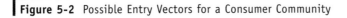

Figure 5-2 Possible Entry Vectors for a Consumer Community

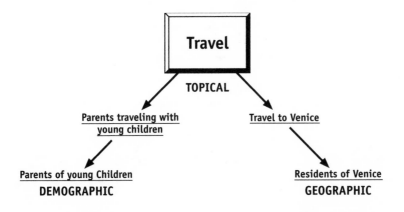

communities will tend to be the stronger consumer entry vectors. They tend to appeal to the largest group of people and have the greater ability to branch out into topical communities. Also, if the degree to which a type of community lends itself to meeting relationship needs is an indicator of future loyalty, then demographic communities in particular, and geographic communities to a lesser extent, are more likely to generate value in the long term. Topical communities may be the hardest entry vector for long-term growth. Although they may inspire great enthusiasm among their members, they are unlikely to meet relational needs in the same way, and they may be too small a base off which to build into demographic and geographic communities.

Topical communities may provide less fertile ground for long-term growth.

There may be some rich yachtsmen in London, but it's hard to imagine a yachting community spawning a London community.

This discussion of near- and longer-term growth rapidly becomes unhelpful if as a community organizer you are trying to assess every possible community to find the single best way to enter this business. It will work better if you have a certain endgame in mind and are trying to figure out the best way to get there. To get to this point requires an assessment of the skills and assets you already own.

Figure 5-3 Possible Entry Vectors for a Business-to-Business Community

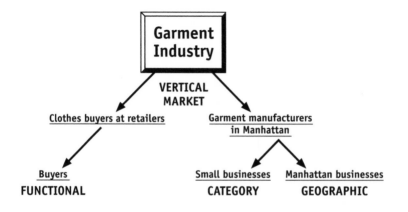

ASSESSING YOUR ABILITY TO OWN A COMMUNITY

For many aspiring community organizers, the decision about which communities to try to organize will be less a function of the communities' long-term economic potential than of their own existing corporate skills and assets. Organizers will need to take this approach cautiously, though. Assets that are valuable in other arenas may be valuable here as well, but new skills will be required to manage them.

The necessary resources

We have not yet discussed the skills required to run a community effectively (we will do so in chapter 7), but there are certain assets that will benefit a community organizer. Since building up a membership base is the first order of the day, the most valuable assets, at least at the start, are those that help an organizer to do this.

Brands. A strong brand carried over to the on-line world can be a very effective tool for attracting browsers to a site. This will be especially true in these early years, when the field will be choked with dozens of players trying to establish the same type of community, and when communities have not yet been able to establish credibility. Many network sites are boldly displaying recognition awards, such as "Top 5% of All Internet Sites" or "Top Shopping Site Award." Consumer goods companies did the same at the end of the nineteenth century, when they displayed on their product labels the awards they had received at international fairs. (Some liquors still do so.) Until communities have established their own brand recognition, long-standing brands, used well, will be powerful assistants in the rush to build a critical mass of members. ESPNET, a sports site that applies community principles more than most, leverages an established brand name from the ESPN cable TV channel. Companies with strong brands should be careful, though, to ensure that the context in which they are used on-line is one they are happy to be associated with.

Customer relationships. Established customer relationships are valuable assets that a company or organization can bring to bear in the early years of building a community. Customer relationships are different from a brand in that they imply a strong understanding of what makes customers tick and an ability to deliver what the customer needs. They also imply an ongoing interaction with customers that could make for an opportunity to introduce them to a newly established virtual community. Prior customer relationships must be actively managed if they are to help establish an on-line site. We will describe in chapter 6 how these prior relationships can be leveraged effectively. For now suffice it to say that they can kick-start a community's growth if leveraged properly. ESPNET can market to its base of committed cable viewers an on-line product that offers features that cannot be obtained from watching TV. This includes access to statistics on demand as well as a forum in which members can create a football team and play it in a fictional league against other knowledgeable, on-line sports fans.

Content. We have maintained that published content will not be the deciding factor in the long run between competing communities. Nevertheless, in the short run, access to published content will be helpful as a draw to lure in browsers, particularly if the content has been adapted to make use of the special capabilities of the on-line world. For example, ESPNET's SportsZone makes ample use of ESPN's stable of recognized sports columnists such as Dick Vitale, Peter Gammons, and Frank Deford (as well as more than sixty other writers). It also leverages ESPN's coverage of every major U.S. sports team and statistics on more than 3,000 professional athletes. This is a powerful draw for U.S. sports fans.

Assets aren't enough

Some communities may have "natural owners" that enter the arena with a strong advantage because of assets such as brand name, deep customer relationships, and, in some cases, published content that they own. Lexis-Nexis understands lawyers, has a strong relationship with a significant portion of all U.S. lawyers, and owns an information service that is indispensable to the lawyers who use it. Disney knows children. It has a globally recognized brand and a unique portfolio of content. Lexis-Nexis and Disney are likely to have a strong head start in the race to establish communities for lawyers and children, respectively, should they choose to do so. But assets alone are insufficient to equip a company to become a community organizer.

We suspect that the *skills* required to organize a community will be as important as any initial advantage a company might appear to have based on its *assets*. If true, this will partially level the playing field and open up the community-organizing business to new competitors.

The keys to becoming a successful organizer over time will be the abilities to aggregate members, retain them, and encourage them to make transactions. Many companies will consider themselves the natural owner of a given type of community. Let's take the "assets" we just listed. There are companies with strong brands, companies with strong customer relationships, companies with strong content. But how relevant are these assets if the company does not know how to spark excitement and grow a community? This is not a product line

Assets alone won't get the job done.

extension, another corporate joint venture, or a different way of packaging the same content. That is precisely the mistake (an understandable one, given the newness of the medium) that so many companies have made in the on-line world. Magazine companies, for instance, have produced on-line magazines, or "Webzines," that fail to encourage communication between "readers"; these companies have forgotten that people don't go on-line just to read. As we mentioned earlier, many corporate sites are glorified posters with little interactivity and, again, no interaction encouraged between customers or between customers and the company. Lack of e-mail, bulletin boards, and chat areas is a clear symptom of a failure to grasp the essentials of what the experience of being on-line can offer.

Why are these things more important than they tend to be in the physical world? Because the on-line world is still chaotic: there are thousands of sites and therefore thousands of "brands," and people browsing do not have the structure they find in their local retail store to guide them to the brands they feel comfortable with. Even the strongest off-line brands can get lost on the Internet, at least for now. The same is true of a strong off-line customer base. While undoubtedly an asset for getting started on-line, a large off-line customer base, transferred on-line without on-line organizing skills, will be as fragmented as the number of access points and destinations on the Internet. Marshaling these resources on-line demands a different set of skills from those developed in the off-line world.

Companies that have desirable assets must therefore focus aggressively on how they will develop or acquire the skills necessary for deploying those assets in organizing virtual communities. We should emphasize that by "skills" we do not mean the technical management of communities, which can be outsourced. What is crucial is the set of skills required to recruit, interest, and serve community members. In some cases this will mean developing the necessary skills internally (which we deal with in greater detail in chapter 7). In others, it will mean partnering with the companies or individuals that have these skills.

In summary, deciding whether to become a community organizer at all depends on whether you have or can develop the skills to build membership quickly and to turn strong off-line content into on-line content that will attract browsers. Deciding then where to compete has two parts. The first is to think about the endgame, which will depend in large measure on the assets a company brings to bear and the relative value of different types of community, such as their size, potential fractal depth, and transaction richness. The second is to assess the fractal breadth of different alternatives, since some pathways in will be more effective than others in establishing a community organizer's future position as a constellation—or even a coalition—organizer.

6

laying the
foundation

getting to critical mass

Establishing a virtual community is a
game of speed and preemption in which
those who move first are likely to enjoy
an enduring advantage. Using other
people's resources can help to accelerate
entry as well as balance urgency with risk.
The primary tasks involved in an effective
entry strategy are to generate,
concentrate, and lock in members quickly.

N OW THAT WE'VE DISCUSSED *WHERE* TO enter the virtual community business, it's time to examine *how* to do so. We'll start with a reminder that increasing returns businesses follow a characteristic pattern marked by an extended ramp-up phase—in which no one has reached critical mass—followed by a sudden spike of accelerated growth for the players that finally do build a big enough customer base to set increasing returns dynamics in motion. Positioning yourself to take advantage of this rapid growth means making your move earlier rather than later. Those who get into increasing returns businesses first are often able to lock in customers and raise entry barriers for the competitors that follow. These dynamics make increasing returns businesses a game of speed and preemption.

Figure 6-1 illustrates the primary challenge confronting organizers as they enter the virtual community business: how to compress the entry period to shorten the near-term profitability squeeze and hit the inflection point in the revenue growth curve sooner rather than later.

Virtual communities bring a new dimension to the increasing returns model. As figure 6-2 shows, building a virtual community requires passing through a series of "gates" to get on the revenue-earning side of the increasing returns trajectory. These gates highlight three broad challenges in building a critical mass of members: generating traffic (getting target community members to travel to your site), concentrating traffic (getting

Community must be in place before commerce can begin.

Figure 6-1 The Entry Challenge: Getting to the Long Term Faster

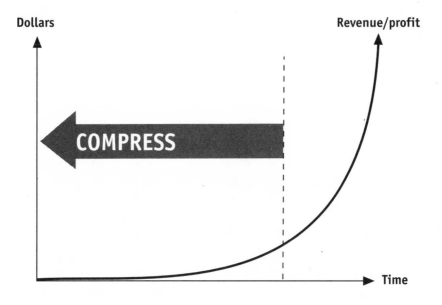

Figure 6-2 The Three Stages of Entry

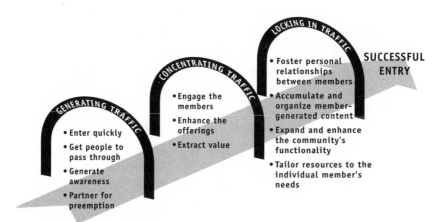

them to spend increasing time in the community), and locking in traffic (creating switching barriers that make it increasingly difficult for members to want to leave the community once they've joined). Until this critical mass has been attained, none of the subsequent revenue-triggering events can occur.

This proposition implies that the rules are different in the virtual environment: traditional blueprints requiring infrastructure investment and a slow buildup of customer base no longer apply. Instead the challenge is to move quickly from a community with no members to a community with a critical mass of members.

To speed up the process, virtual community organizers will do well to rely on leveraged entry strategies. These allow the organizer to concentrate resources on the acquisition of community members by "piggybacking" on the content and technology that's already on the network. Leveraged strategies are particularly well suited to network environments, especially open-network platforms like the Internet, where you can build on the efforts of others while focusing your own resources to achieve maximum leverage and speed.

STAGE ONE: GENERATING TRAFFIC

Nothing's more uninviting to passing Web traffic than a community without members. Witness the difficulty Apple experienced with the introduction of e-World. Praised for its engaging graphics and well-organized environments, e-World soon became known on the Net as "Empty World"—in reference to the frustration of early members who eagerly entered chat rooms only to find they were the only ones there, or who ventured onto bulletin boards only to find they were invited to make the first entry.

At the opposite end of the spectrum, few things are more attractive to passers-by than a community with a critical mass of members. Members enter the community and find hundreds of bulletin boards covering every topic imaginable with lots of recent postings, they enter crowded chat rooms and encounter diverse and interesting people, they review crowded special events calendars featuring many well-known experts in their field, and they see an abundance of content provided by major publishers. Organizers find themselves riding the wave of increasing returns that rapidly increases barriers to entry and boosts profitability. But how do you get to a critical mass of members?

Enter quickly

Advice to enter the virtual community business quickly may be self-evident, but if rigorously observed, it can lead to some important implications for strategy. If "Speed is God, and time is the devil," then anything that consumes time before entry must be sharply questioned and anything that accelerates entry should be eagerly evaluated. Traditional corporate wisdom that one must have a detailed blueprint before undertaking a major business initiative is just one example of practices that may work in other business environments but are likely to lead to real trouble in increasing returns businesses. Even if there were enough certainty to permit a detailed blueprint to be developed plausibly, the time consumed in such an enterprise would significantly increase the risk of preemption. Instead, what management may need are a few basic principles to guide day-to-day decision making and tight information feedback mechanisms to learn what is working and what is not.

Accelerating entry means taking a pragmatic view of technology platforms: whatever is available off the shelf has a big advantage over any technological option that needs development. Any community initiative that includes substantial technological innovation as part of its game plan is suspect: technology innovation takes time, consumes resources, and increases uncertainty. The technological aspects of the virtual community business are discussed in chapter 8.

Get people to pass through

In the early days of community formation, the key imperative is to generate traffic. Too often, community organizers think they must have a rich set of resources available on their site before they can start to generate traffic. But this is to fail to take advantage of the power of the network. This is also to run the serious risk of delaying entry while the "necessary" resources are being developed.

The power of the network available to community organizers is that which allows them to leverage each other's efforts in building their new communities. One obvious way to do this is to begin simply by offering a directory to other resources on the network that would be of interest to target community members. This kind of directory may be especially valuable to target community members if it offers evaluations or ratings of potential resources as well as thoughtful tips on how such resources might be used.

Piggyback to get started.

Consider the example of a planned virtual community for people who run businesses out of their home. One might start such a community by surveying the Internet to find all the resources useful to target members: marketing information sources that help people to target potential customers, information on home office products (photo-copiers, fax machines, telephone systems, personal computers, sta-tionery), information on filing various kinds of tax forms, and potential sources of financing. Since the prospective members of this community are busy people, trying to get the most out of each minute, a compre-hensive directory service that evaluates the various sources of informa-tion would be valuable to them. The value proposition is to ensure that members get both breadth (all the resources potentially relevant) and depth (guidance to the specific resources that are likely to be most useful).

Such an approach has five advantages:

1. It significantly accelerates entry. Once the directory is developed (using search engine technology that is readily available from a number of suppliers), the initiative can be launched and begin to start building a presence.

2. It reduces the need for heavy investment in content at the outset by leveraging the investments in content that others have made.

3. It begins to build a brand image among target community members as a guide that can be relied on to direct them to the most relevant and highest quality resources on the network.

4. It gets target community members in the habit of coming to the site whenever they have a need relevant to the community, even if they are only passing through on their way to other sites suggested by the directory.

5. It provides the community organizer with valuable information about the interests and needs of target community members. By tracking the topics most requested and the rates of repeat usage, the organizer can begin to prioritize the distinctive offerings that the community should develop over time.

In this early stage of community formation, it is not essential for target community members to stay at the site. The most important challenge is to maximize the traffic to the site. Once you have people coming to your site, you are well positioned to merchandise additional commu-nity offerings as they become available.

One obvious extension of the first directory offering is to put up bulletin boards where users can return to post their comments on the sites mentioned in the directory as well as to suggest additional sites.

This begins to leverage the contributions of potential community members and starts to address the primary values of virtual communities—members exchanging information among themselves on topics of common interest.

In general, the directory approach highlights one of the key principles of community entry strategies: minimize early investment in published content. Those who don't will only increase their financial exposure, while also creating significant lead-time before entry and shifting focus away from the key challenge—generating traffic to the site. Leveraging the published content of others through such devices as directories and search engines is only one approach to minimizing dependence on published content in the early stage of community development. Other approaches include leveraging member contributions through aggressive deployment of bulletin boards and chat environments, recruiting of "magnet" personalities/authorities to seed the community, and, where appropriate, selectively deploying "anchor" content already owned by the community organizers (for instance, magazines, newsletters, or Yellow Pages directories with strong brand recognition that have the ability to "pull" in both target community members and other published content providers over time).

In focusing on accelerating traffic generation, carefully evaluate any registration programs or member fees. Both of these have so far demonstrated a significant power to reduce traffic to Internet sites. Registration programs are important vehicles through which to identify community members, but the value of the information must be carefully weighed against the adverse impact on traffic generation, especially in the first stage of community formation. Where necessary, registration programs should be kept very simple and be easy to complete. The dilemma regarding member fees has already been described (see chapter 3). The temptation to capture near-term revenue generation opportunities must be carefully weighed against the significant dampening effect on traffic generation.

Generate awareness

As the resources available on the network multiply, generating awareness of an emerging community becomes more and more challenging. As the marketing efforts of many network-based businesses expand, generating this awareness with minimal investment becomes even more difficult. Even so, there are many things a community organizer can do to target and develop awareness among potential community members without pouring money into conventional advertising.

The real focus of community organizers should be to leverage existing information networks that permeate the nonnetwork-based community. Almost any virtual community that is likely to be built on electronic networks has some analogs in physical space. These existing communities often have well-developed information networks, whether it be in the form of word-of-mouth news at meetings or of newsletters and magazines. On-line community organizers need to find the most powerful influencers in these existing information networks, those people who are "well connected." The head of an industry association, the organizer of an annual conference, or a widely read newsletter editor might be such influencers.

The goal should be to develop targeted programs that create a "buzz" and an impression of significant momentum among these community influencers. Often this can be accomplished through regular briefings that highlight accomplishments of the virtual community. VIP membership programs might be helpful in encouraging these influencers to experience the community firsthand. Advisory boards might be established to involve these influencers in shaping the virtual community and to communicate a sense of momentum to broader members of the community. The conventional media (newsletters, magazines, radio and TV programs) that are most targeted to broader members of the community should be encouraged to provide regular coverage of the virtual community. Traditional gatherings of the target community (industry association meetings, trade shows, "club" meetings) should be persuaded to feature sessions on the virtual community and the services it offers. In some cases, formal affiliations with existing industry associations or hobbyist groups can be used to leverage the recognition and credibility already established by these groups.

Virtual community organizers also need to be thoughtful about capturing the attention of potential members who might already be on-line. What sites are these potential members most likely to visit? Contacting these sites and developing reciprocal links with them can be a useful way to increase visibility and generate an impression of momentum. Find the directories that potential community members are most likely to access and ensure that the virtual community is prominently and accurately featured there.

Finally, virtual community organizers should aggressively leverage any existing media and marketing programs that they may already have in related businesses. For example, organizers who come to the virtual community business from a traditional publishing background should be heavily featuring the virtual community in related media and advertising. Adopting a name for the virtual community that builds on well-established brand names already owned by the organizer may also be helpful. Where relevant, community memberships might be included in bundles with traditional products and services the organizer offers already.

Partner for preemption

Given the significant strategic value in accelerating member acquisition, community organizers should carefully consider the role of partnerships they might enter into with three kinds of companies. These partnerships may significantly contribute to the preemptive acquisition of members by helping to acquire the assets described in chapter 5. They may take a variety of forms, ranging from loose commercial relationships—where the community organizer pays the marketing "partner" a bounty or finder's fee for each member the community signs up—to much more formal and permanent joint ventures with shared equity investment by the community organizer and one or more partners.

The first category of company to consider for partnership is that with strong distribution capability. These companies, which are characterized by strong brand recognition, existing customer relationships, and well-established off-line sales and distribution capabilities targeted at potential community members, may be able to reach and recruit potential members quickly. While attractive from a marketing point of view, however, these companies may be difficult in that they often have a vested interest in reaching community members on their own terms and may be reluctant to create any environment where other vendors can reach the same audience on a level playing field. For example, a geographically oriented virtual community organizer might be tempted to partner with a local bank, but the bank may be reluctant to allow competing banks to gain access to the community.

To get around this problem, look for a partner that has a strong brand image with target community members but that operates in a category of products or services unrelated to the community's focus. For example, Fidelity Investments might make an interesting partner for the organizer of a travel community targeting affluent travelers, while American Express might make an interesting partner for a personal stock investment community organizer. Alternatively, look for a partner that acts as a traditional intermediary (say, a retailer or distributor), covering product areas that are directly related to the focus of the community but that the community organizer cannot provide.

A second category of company to consider is closely related to the first. It consists of owners of the kind of "anchor" published content that has great power to draw other participants into the community and that is difficult to replicate. In this category, the goal is to find published content that can serve to accelerate member acquisition rather than simply round out the content portfolio offered by the community. These companies often create the same difficulty as those in the first category—reluctance to give competing content providers access to the virtual community.

For example, in the travel community discussed in chapter 3, the community organizer might want to line up American Express as a partner, in part because it publishes *Travel & Leisure*, one of the leading special-interest travel magazines. But how willing would American Express be to have material from a competing magazine like *Condé Nast Traveler* appear in the community? This resistance might be overcome if it could be convinced that offering more than one travel magazine would actually draw a much broader audience for *Travel & Leisure* than any community limited to one magazine. In this example, American Express also has other travel-related businesses that might make it willing to endure some increased competition at the magazine level in return for the ability to participate in the much broader range of business opportunities created by the community.

A third category of company involves potential competitors. Who else might organize a similarly focused virtual community, and what is their relative strength in reaching and recruiting target members? These competitors might come from existing organizations already serving the target community in some way in physical space, or they may come from unexpected quarters—even from someone who has set up shop in their garage down the block. The challenge is to scan the landscape, identify potential competitors, and realistically assess their ability to build comparable communities.

Once again, the primary focus should be on competitors with highly developed member acquisition assets or capabilities rather than competitors with resources that would be interesting to community members. Where these competitors potentially exist, it may make more sense to partner with them even before they launch their virtual community initiatives to neutralize the competitive threat and to leverage their member acquisition capabilities rather than to go head to head with them.

STAGE TWO: CONCENTRATING TRAFFIC

The second stage of virtual community formation involves concentrating traffic in the community. At this point, it is no longer sufficient for target members merely to travel through the site. It is now essential to create incentives for people to spend increasing time in there. In truth, this stage overlaps with the first—as soon as some people start visiting the community, the organizer should work to keep them there. This is a prerequisite for a related business challenge at this stage—extracting economic value from community members.

Increasing member usage rates is important for several reasons. First, it enables the community organizer to develop a much more detailed profile of community members to learn more precisely what would be most valuable to them. This in turn permits more accurate targeting of merchandising and advertising messages. It also increases the ability of the community organizer to attract relevant content providers and vendors, both because there is a more sustained audience or market for them and because there is more information about the audience or market. Finally, increasing usage rates also helps to create the conditions for the third stage of community development: raising switching barriers.

Broadly speaking, the three major goals of traffic concentration are to engage members, enhance their experience, and extract economic value from services rendered to them.

Engage members

Engaging members involves tracking usage patterns and soliciting direct input from members to determine what will make the experience in the community more compelling for them. The more compelling the experience, the more likely they are to return frequently and to spend more time on each visit.

A more compelling experience could involve tailoring the individual member's view of the community to his or her interests. This involves analyzing usage patterns to determine which parts of the community the member tends to spend time in and tailoring the member's entry path so that those parts appear immediately on entry or so that the information that is most relevant to the member appears at the top of a page rather than buried at the bottom.

The risk of taking this approach is that the community becomes ever more narrowly defined for each member based on prior preferences and the pleasure of unexpectedly coming across something of interest is lost. This risk can be reduced by the use of agent technology like Firefly (developed by Agents, Inc.), which compares usage profiles of members and, on the basis of this information, suggests other dimensions of the community a member might find valuable because members with comparable usage profiles seem to enjoy them.

Another way to make the community more compelling is to create experiences that address as many of the four needs driving community formation as possible: information, transaction, fantasy, and relationship. The latter two needs—fantasy and relationship—in particular appear to drive very high usage levels. Some communities, such as medieval fantasy gaming or disability communities, are naturally positioned to target these needs. On the other hand, even rather different kinds of communities may be able to tap into these needs quite effectively. For example, a community for lawyers might be able to develop litigation strategy "games" in which lawyers can compete and develop their skills in trial tactics. A community of Civil War enthusiasts might offer a bulletin board that helps sponsors of Civil War battle recreations find volunteers to participate in these recreations and, in the process, lead to the creation of personal relationships.

Bulletin boards and chat areas are the elements of the community most effective in engaging members. A virtuous cycle is often unleashed once members start contributing to these areas of the community. The act of contributing creates a feeling of involvement and ownership that draws members in more tightly to the community and motivates them to contribute even more actively over time. Transforming members from "lurkers," who simply observe as others

Building community means turning "lurkers" into contributors.

contribute to the development of the community, into active contributors is an important task for the community organizer. In part this can be accomplished by more actively promoting the range of member participation opportunities available. It may also be possible to create incentives for participation by adding areas that are accessible only to active contributors or by offering special discounts on products and services to active contributors.

Often, the process of more effectively engaging members may be as simple as monitoring member support bulletin boards to determine which elements of the design and environment are least intuitive or comfortable for members. This can give organizers valuable insight into how they might refine the broader community architecture to make it easier and more comfortable to use. It may involve developing different areas in the community to accommodate both novices and veterans.

Enhance the offerings

Community organizers must be aggressive in expanding the range of offerings available to community members. The challenge is to continue to enhance the range and depth of offerings to create incentives for members to return, both because there is more to do and because there is a sense of excitement relating to the fact that members never know what will now be available.

The range of offerings is a function both of contributions by members themselves and of efforts to recruit new content providers and vendors to participate in the community. Community organizers should aggressively canvas members to identify suggestions for related content, products, and services they would find helpful. One important function of directories is to give organizers insight into what community members are seeking. Frequency of search requests can be an important indicator of unmet demand. Similarly, bulletin boards that ask members to identify and rate other communities they access on the network can provide valuable information on member interests and needs. Another indicator may be members' sites of origin—where were they immediately before they came to the community site?

Community organizers should also make it easy and attractive for vendors to approach and participate in the community. The awareness-building programs discussed in stage one above serve a dual function: they attract new members, and they attract new vendors. Detailed aggregate profiles of community membership should be available and packaged to persuade specific categories of vendors that the community offers an attractive environment in which they can reach target customers and position their offerings. Content development tool kits can help to reduce barriers preventing providers from posting their content in the community.

Understanding the economics of various vendor types can also be helpful in fashioning appropriate relationships with vendors to maximize their incentive to participate in the community. For example, CD-ROM publishers experience high distribution and marketing costs because of limited retail shelf space and few venues for product trial by potential customers (CD music producers have radio and MTV). Knowing this, a community organizer targeting the gaming interests of teenagers might be able to make an attractive pitch to CD-ROM publishers regarding the advantages of on-line communities as a distribution channel.

In attracting new providers to the community, organizers must carefully balance their interest in broadening offerings to community members with their need to protect the community's reputation for guaranteeing the quality of its resources. Expanding offerings too rapidly and thereby eroding a reputation for quality can be a shortsighted strategy. Community organizers should be thoughtful about the use of admission criteria, rating systems, and levels of participation as ways of balancing the need for breadth and quality.

In expanding the range of offerings, community organizers should pay particular attention to the role of "special events." These can take many forms. They might be scheduled (or even impromptu) chat sessions with experts or personalities known to members. They might be member contests or "challenges." They might even be "sales" on products or services offered within the community. The point is to surprise and delight members with unexpected events and to provide incentives for them to return frequently because events occur at specific times.

The other dimension of enhancing offerings is to deepen existing ones. This focuses on the specific "fractal" nature of community evolution discussed in chapter 5 that permits, and even demands, much more depth as membership grows. The leading edge of depth is typically in the bulletin boards and chat areas where the alert community organizer will start to see subdiscussions emerge repeatedly around more narrowly defined topics, often driven by one or two members who have particular passion about or expertise in these topics. For example, a scuba diving community might find a group of members who are particularly interested in sharing experiences and information about cave diving, a highly specialized form of scuba diving.

As clusters start to form, suggesting broader interest in these narrowly defined topics, community organizers can begin to cultivate "kernels" of new bulletin boards or chat areas, often led by the members who started to generate interest in this topic in broader discussion areas. As these more narrowly defined bulletin boards or chat areas begin to take shape and acquire a critical mass of members, the community organizer can recruit related providers to participate in these emerging subcommunities.

Extract value

Commercial virtual communities must ultimately develop business models that reward the community organizer and the providers of content, goods, and services to the community for bringing value to community members. The engine that drives this value extraction will be the profiles of member activities. These profiles provide a powerful mechanism for targeting messages on items of value to community members and for recruiting providers who are interested in reaching people who fit a certain profile. Over time, another powerful engine might be the accumulation of vendor profiles that could be marketed to members.

Community organizers must be sure to capture, organize, and use this information in such a way that maximizes its economic value without violating the privacy concerns of members. The long-term value of this information to the organizers hinges on their ability to use it responsibly in delivering value to members.

For example, the community organizer can serve as a helpful filter for members, ensuring that only advertisements or commercial messages truly relevant to the member will reach that member. A torrent of "junk" e-mail is the surest way to trigger privacy concerns and an information collection backlash among members. In fact, successful community organizers will be able to structure involvement in a community so that members can specify the level and type of advertising they wish to receive and help members to evaluate the qualifications of specific vendors seeking to reach them. Those who do not want to receive any advertising may be able to participate in the community but pay higher member fees than those who are more willing to receive advertising relevant to their needs.

Community organizers can also begin to perform an agent function for members. By thoughtfully analyzing members' activity profiles, organizers can begin to spot opportunities to solicit information that might be of interest to members. For example, a member of an audiophile community who starts reading information in the community about how to evaluate high-end speakers for cars might find it helpful to receive product information about various types of high-end speakers. By identifying vendors selling appropriate speakers and coupling product information from them with a convenient way to order the speakers, the community organizer may be able to capture both advertising and transaction revenues—while at the same time performing a useful service for the community member.

As indicated in the previous chapter, extracting value from the community will ultimately involve some combination of member fees, advertising revenues, and transaction commissions. This combination, and the overall value extraction potential, will depend on the nature of the virtual community. The key to success will be to leverage member profiles in a responsible way that takes into account the nature of the community and that delivers tangible value to members as well as value to the providers seeking to reach those members.

STAGE THREE: LOCKING IN TRAFFIC

In this stage, the key focus is to create switching barriers that make it increasingly difficult over time for members to want to leave the community and join a competing community.

Foster personal relationships between members

Bulletin boards and chat areas are particularly powerful in terms of their ability to build personal relationships within a community. The more a member gets to know fellow members "Joe" or "Mary" and comes to rely on them for advice and counsel, the more difficult it will be for the member to switch to a competing community. Even if that competing community has bulletin boards and chat areas on exactly the same topics, they are unlikely to offer access to "Joe" or "Mary." Particular relationships will be unique to the individual community.

Community organizers should do more to address members' need for relationship than promote bulletin boards and chat areas. Certain virtual communities, such as disease communities (cancer, diabetes), dependency communities (alcoholism, addiction), and personal trauma communities (divorce, widows/widowers), inevitably foster deep personal relationships. However, even topical communities can promote the creation of personal relationships. For example, a sports community might sponsor member outings to local sports events, create "dating" bulletin boards, or give members access to one another's profiles (if members authorize them to do so) to help them find people who share interests other than sports. All of these devices will help to address the personal relationship needs of community members. The more these needs are met within a specific community, the more difficult it will be for members to leave that community.

> *Members will create their own reasons not to leave a community.*

Accumulate and organize member-generated content

Member-generated content—the accumulated postings to bulletin boards and the transcripts of chat—is an asset unique to each community. If members leave that community, they may find similar categories of member-generated content in other communities, but they will not find that same content. By rapidly accumulating this kind of content, aggressively editing it to maintain high standards of quality, and by indexing the content to make it easily accessible in response to future member needs, the community organizer will be strengthening a unique asset. That asset serves to differentiate the community and will make it harder for members who rely on access to it to leave.

Improve community functionality

Community organizers can aggressively leverage another unique asset—usage profiles of members—to address member needs preemptively. By watching for the emergence of discussion clusters around specific subtopics in bulletin boards and chat areas, for instance, community organizers can rapidly build out service offerings. This fractal depth will increase members' reluctance to move to other communities that have been less aggressive in building out their offerings.

Raising switching barriers in this case may not require expanding offerings, but simply picking up cues from usage patterns on how to develop more user-friendly interfaces and designs. For example, a community organizer might determine that members ask for information on a certain topic by specifying a key word that is not effectively captured in the community's current indexing scheme. By making a series of minor improvements like this, the community organizer can convey the sense that "things are just easier to find in this community," and that will tend to keep members locked in and reluctant to switch.

Tailor resources to individual member needs

Another way to leverage the unique asset of member usage profiles will be to invest in technologies that allow the organizer or, increasingly, the community members to tailor the community experience to meet their individual needs. For example, community members might be able to customize their user interface or the directories they access to reflect their preferences or priorities. Long-time community members might find the menu screens designed to help new members navigate through the community too time consuming. They might specify a set of initial screens presenting choices of the forums, vendors, and information services they visit most frequently and resort to the more comprehensive menus only on the infrequent occasions that they seek out something new. Communities might provide each member with a tailored newsletter each time they enter the community that highlights items likely to be of interest given each member's previous activity and interest patterns. Technology is available to monitor which items in such a newsletter the community member selects to read in more detail and based on that information can further refine the selection of future newsletter items.

Members might be provided with agent technology they could train to reflect their preferences. For example, a purchasing department manager for a fast-food restaurant chain might be provided by a food service community with agent technology to search out the best new suppliers of potatoes. Based on prior purchasing patterns, this agent technology would "know" that the purchasing manager wants a specific quality of potato from a limited number of geographic areas and will deal only with vendors able to meet certain terms on delivery and payment schedules. The agent technology would then search out appropriate vendors and seek out bids for the supplies required. By recording what choice the purchasing manager makes among the bids presented, the agent technology would refine its search criteria for the next round of purchases. This accumulated insight into the needs and preferences of the purchasing manager becomes valuable to him. He would probably be loath to lose it by trading this community for another.

This customization may require some investment of time initially by community members, but it will significantly enhance their experiences in the community, and once done it will make them more reluctant to switch. Any new community will lack the usage profile required for the community organizer to help members tailor the environment to their needs, and members themselves will face the time-consuming task of adapting the environment to reflect their needs.

Entering the virtual community business involves a fair degree of risk and uncertainty. By piggybacking on the prior investments of others, however, and by keeping a single-minded focus on building a critical mass of members before beginning to worry about commerce, organizers can enter the virtual community business quickly and effectively. These actions will also make them less vulnerable to attack by the competitors who come along later.

7

the
gardener's
touch
managing organic growth

Throw out the spreadsheets, blueprints,
organization charts, and five-year plans.
Virtual communities require a new mindset
and a fresh managerial approach—more
like the gardener's methods of seeding,
feeding, and weeding. Successful
organizers will balance an organic
approach to community building with a
tight focus on the key economic levers
that drive value creation.

WHAT DOES THE VIRTUAL COMMUNITY organizer do when the hoped-for success of the community brings with it an increasingly large number of members? After all, it isn't easy to feel a sense of community in a large crowd of people. That's why, when thinking about what's required to manage and organize a virtual community as it grows, organizers must build an organization that is "scalable" enough to allow the community as a whole to benefit as its membership increases into the thousands and perhaps even millions. What this means is that the community organizer must preserve community members' sense of intimacy and continuity while also capturing the benefits of scale that can be passed on—at least in part—to members.

At an abstract level, managing a community effectively will be exactly like managing any other business: setting the right performance measures—and adapting them as the business grows—will be an important lever to use in making sure the community remains healthy. But once you examine the specifics, it is clear that the managerial challenges of organizing a virtual community require a different, more organic approach than is required by most other businesses. In this chapter we examine these managerial challenges and suggest that the gardener's skills of seeding, feeding, and weeding are the most analogous to those community organizers will need to help virtual communities grow. We also take a look at the new skills and organizational roles that are essential to the community's success.

GROWTH REQUIREMENTS

Growth of the virtual community depends on the organizer's ability to do two things: (1) provide scalability, which allows a community to grow without losing its sense of community, and (2) let go, which means allowing a community grow organically without being "overplanned" or "overmanaged."

Providing scalability

We're often asked how many people will be able to join a community before it begins to lose its sense of *being* a community. Our answer is that we believe virtual communities as we have defined them (made up of large numbers of subcommunities) have the potential to grow into the millions of members. In other words, we believe that communities are "scalable"—that they can enjoy the benefits of growth while they also maintain a sense of community. These two aims need not be mutually exclusive, but the community organizer must take active steps to make this possibility a reality.

Preserve the sense of community. There are two aspects of community preservation. First, the organizer must structure the community to preserve its intimacy. Once a sense of community has been developed, it can easily dissolve if the small groups of which it is comprised are overwhelmed by too many newcomers. For a virtual community to preserve its sense of community, its subcommunities must remain small. There are a couple of ways to accomplish this, neither of which will occur on their own. The organizer must make them happen.

First, the community organizer can work to establish a culture that encourages the development of new, fractal subcommunities once enough members indicate a specialized interest through what they say or look for on bulletin boards or in chat areas. To do this, the organizer must give subcommunities the resources they need to develop. The philosophy of growth must be explained to members as they join and reinforced among community managers (the role of community managers is discussed later in the chapter) so that they are on the lookout for opportunities to help subcommunities form. On AOL, for example, chat rooms are limited to twenty-five people. If a twenty-sixth person tries to enter, a new chat room is established. The same principles could apply to subcommunities, which will include not only chat rooms, of course, but bulletin boards, on-line events, advertising, and transactions as well.

Second, the organizer can establish "tiering" within subcommunities that allows stalwarts to enjoy some protection from hordes of "newbies." A delicate balance must be struck between ensuring the "quality" of members and encouraging all newcomers to join in. The nature of the balance is likely to differ by community type. A geographic community targeted at people who have recently moved into an area may be more open to participation by all than a community where sophisticated investment techniques are debated. Even within a type of community, the rigor of the filter applied to new members could vary considerably, and members would be free to choose communities with filters that meet their needs. It is possible that communities will segment into zones, some of which are accessible to all and some of which have controls on access. Sometimes a compromise is offered. In Silicon Investor, one of the sites we described in chapter 5, there is an area called Stock Talk, described as "a forum for educated analysis and discussion of the tech industry. As a registered user, you can participate in the daily discussions. Otherwise, you are always welcome to learn and observe from the sidelines." Access is open, participation is somewhat limited.

The second important aspect of community preservation is maintaining its integrity, or a sense of continuity among members. Churn is a major issue for many Internet start-ups. There is so much that is new to explore that surfers on the network keep moving on to other sites. To preserve community, the organizer must try to encourage the same people to keep coming back. One way to do this is to offer a calendar of events, which act as "hooks" to draw members back often enough to start developing relationships with others in the community. Establishing directories, along the lines described in chapter 6, can at least draw people back to the community as a starting point to their on-line explorations. Careful merchandising efforts, possibly combined with customized agenting tools that know what products to search for on the member's behalf, form another mechanism that can encourage members to keep coming back, the appeal being the compelling transactions they are offered.

Ensure that advantages of scale are captured. At the same time that a community organizer is helping each subcommunity to remain intimate, it must also capture the benefits of scale and make sure the broader community enjoys them. A larger community will have negotiating power that a smaller community does not. The community organizer must make sure that its managers take advantage of this clout across the board as they negotiate the cost of rights to published content, as they invite famous guests, and as they purchase software or bargain on prices of goods and services.

A larger community will be able to spread major expenses across a larger base of members, but it must make sure subcommunities draw on centralized resources rather than staffing up for themselves. Shared expenses could include marketing, customer service, information systems, information management, and billing.

Letting go

The second requirement for successful growth is a loose hand on the reins. A community will not grow if the organizer tries to maintain too much control over ownership, leadership, content, community structure, and management decisions.

Create franchises. We have suggested that an organizer be on the lookout for opportunities to create subcommunities. Taking this a step further, an organizer should be flexible enough to allow communities to be "hived off" as franchises (or affiliates, as described in chapter 4), giving their managers a stake in ownership while keeping subcommunities within the parent (or core) community's sphere of influence. This is not unlike the concept practiced by Bloomingdale's department stores, which rent out space to independent retailers who benefit from the consistent environment of the store and yet maintain independent ownership and management.

The managers of a "franchised" subcommunity could control its design and its daily operations. But there will be limits to the degree of control the organizer should give up. It will be especially important for a parent community to preserve the right to capture information on member activity in all of its subcommunities. It should also ensure that members can access subcommunities only from within the parent community (as opposed to directly from the Internet, for example). The parent community must find ways to keep members of a subcommunity tied emotionally to the parent, possibly by encouraging members of the parent and franchise to spend time in each other's areas.

Empower members. A community organizer should empower members when it comes to decisions about how their community should look, who markets to them, and what they say to each other. But the organizer must strike a balance between member empowerment and protection of the broader community's interests. The organizer should step in to preserve the rights of the majority—and to maintain the quality of the site. Many on-line sites are open about their right to silence obnoxious participants—a problem more likely to occur in a consumer community than in one focused on business. Members should also be encouraged to participate actively in the community, performing leadership roles in subcommunities. Again, this is a culture that must constantly be reinforced among both members and managers: leaders must be actively identified and equipped.

An "organic" management model

For a community to grow, we believe, its managers and overseers must develop a mindset that is very unlike that required in other businesses. We have already discussed the concept of "natural owners"—existing businesses that seem to be natural candidates for virtual community organizer. And we've said that many who believe their preexisting assets position them well for this kind of natural ownership may in fact be in for an unpleasant surprise when these assets turn out to be less important than the mindset and skills the company brings to the enterprise. The best way to characterize this mindset is "organic."

As anyone who has already started a business on-line can attest, a community's growth cannot be "planned" to the same extent that a new food product's launch can be organized on the basis of a five-year plan. These plans can be a trap for the community organizer. While a certain degree of planning is responsible, the directions a community takes as it grows will likely be difficult to forecast with precision, since they will be a function not only of who participates but also of the chemistry between participants.

> *The best-laid plans are often the worst.*

A community will constantly evolve: unlike most other products—but like other creative media—a community will mutate as it grows. As discussed in chapter 5, points of interest to certain groups of members will crop up, creating opportunities for subcommunities to develop if the organizer is alert to the opportunity and supplies the necessary resources. It is just this kind of naturally evolving growth that is desirable. These subcommunities—and so the community overall—will be much more successful than if they had been planned.

Parent Soup, the emerging parenting community described in chapter 5, encourages members to suggest new on-line "groups": "Can't find the group you need? Start your own. To get your group started, go to our Bulletin Boards . . . post a message describing the purpose of your group and when you'd like to meet. Then we'll help you get the ball rolling." Managers must release control to the customer. The customer, in this case more than any other, must truly define the product.

Managing a community's growth involves seeding, feeding, and weeding. *Seeding* can refer to the experiment of starting up new subcommunities and then waiting to see if they work, much as Sony at one point invested in new product development by throwing money at many projects and waiting to see which ones "stuck to the wall." The Sony Walkman was the result. An on-line example is AOL's "Greenhouse" effort to cultivate the development of subcommunities. AOL provides seed money for entrepreneurs to develop virtual community business concepts and assists them with on-line production support, marketing resources, and on-line promotion. This has resulted in the launch of several successful community-type concepts, such as Motley Fool, HouseNet, Thrive (a health- and fitness-related topical area), NetNoir (for African Americans), and iSKI. Within a community, seeding means starting conversations by planting provocative ideas, finding engaging or celebrity hosts, and recruiting enthusiastic members. Sometimes these subcommunities will emerge and develop on their own, but often they must be actively fostered.

Feeding means that promising subcommunities must be given resources to find and support vendors, to create or buy access to published content where it is felt to be of value, and to invest in chat hosting, customer service, and supporting systems. The community organizer must create a management environment in which risk taking is welcomed and rewarded if it is responsive to members' needs. Feeding also refers to the encouragement a community organizer should give to creative and energetic organizers of subcommunities, even if some of their efforts result in failure. These individuals will be crucial to a community's long-term vigor.

Weeding means that the community's managers must constantly be on the lookout for "dead wood" to prune. For instance, empty chat rooms should be removed or changed because they diminish the sense of community and dampen enthusiasm. Obnoxious behavior by advertisers or members should be controlled. Unpopular on-line events should be phased out. Organizers of subcommunities who are not responsive to members' needs should be replaced. But weeding should not be imposed on community members arbitrarily. It must not be perceived as heavy-handed. For example, one way to phase out stagnant or uneconomical areas of the community is to set a predetermined time limit on the life of all subcommunities or individual chat areas and to reevaluate their continuation at that time.

Overall responsibility for running a community of the size and nature described in chapter 3 (including oversight of functions such as marketing, content development, and financial management) is not for your traditional general manager. What's required is a blend of creativity, flexibility, and (given the community's size) financial rigor. It is not unlike that of a producer in a movie studio. In fact, the person who fills the chief operating role for Parent Soup describes herself as its producer.

A community's executive producer must have an eye for the creative, a feel for the community member, an instinct for drawing "talent" to the community, and a handle on the bottom line. A strong sense of timing will be crucial. For example, it will be up to the executive producer to decide when the community should start expanding its focus from acquiring members to increasing usage and attracting advertisers and vendors. The executive producer must know when to intervene and when to let things take their course. The producer must balance flexibility and control.

SKILL REQUIREMENTS

One of an executive producer's key roles will be to find and develop the skills required to grow the community. Each stage of community development has a different skill set associated with it. Many of the roles required to manage a community are new, while others are variants on roles that are played in business enterprises today. (Figure 7-1 lays out an organization chart for a midsized to large community.) These roles fall naturally into the three areas of activity they are

net gain |

associated with: acquiring members, stimulating usage, and extracting value from the community.

Figure 7-1 Organization Chart for an Established Community

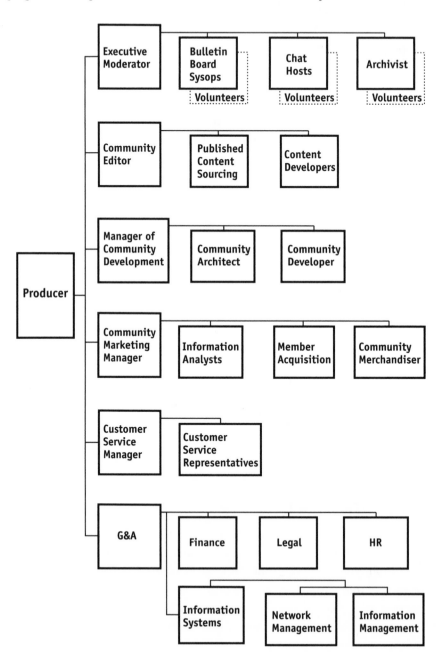

Member acquisition

Responsibility for reaching out to potential members essentially falls to the community marketing manager. This has a clearly measurable performance goal: an expected number of new members. The marketer can leverage member information profiles as well as subjective feedback from chat areas and bulletin boards to learn what elements of the community current participants value most.

Using a data set that is richer than most marketers now use, a community marketer can apply the traditional skills of marketing analysis to segment the community's "market" and develop a message to attract potential members.

"Buzz" is the fuel of on-line marketing.

Communicating the message will require some new approaches. The marketer will have limited access to traditional media for advertising purposes, at least in the near term, because of the expense. Marketing a community is about creating a buzz to encourage free PR and stimulate word of mouth. It is also about knowing where to advertise on-line and how to promote the community through trade and other associations.

Member usage

There is a string of roles required to stimulate usage of a community by its members, once they have made the decision to try it out.

Host. Hosts manage member-generated content, which includes bulletin boards, chat areas, and real-time on-line events. We'll describe three forms of hosts, two of which exist today. One is the bulletin board "sysop" (system operator) that we mentioned earlier in the book. There are an estimated 40,000 of these in the United States. Sysops manage a specific bulletin board with varying degrees of editorial control, depending on the philosophy of the community. They can ensure that no "unsuitable" questions or answers are posted—meaning those which are "repetitive," "in error," or "not in good taste." (The definitions of these are in the sysop's hands, not Webster's dictionary.)

A second role is that of chat host, who moderates real-time chat areas. The term is an accepted one in general use today. Chat hosts perform the same editorial role as sysops, but participate in the conversation, seeding it with interesting questions or ideas. They can be the hosts of the party and its bouncers. Chat hosts are a cross between a newspaper columnist and a talk-show host. They and the sysops are likely in future to become more "activist" in their approach to ensuring a high quality of conversations and member interactions, especially as communities grow and large numbers of new members come on-line.

Many sysops and chat hosts are community members who work in their roles on a volunteer basis, generally receiving compensation in the form of free usage in return for their time. In addition to these two positions, there may eventually be a need for an executive moderator who has responsibility for all member-generated content. This person would oversee the hosts and sysops, recruiting them, training them, vetting them, and performing routine quality control of their work. This itself will require an organic approach to management: the moderator must learn to identify the qualities of an effective host or sysop, wait for good ones to emerge, and give them a role in a subcommunity. This is bound to take time, and good chat hosts may become a valuable resource. One Silicon Valley company, LiveWorld (established by the former manager of Apple's eWorld, Peter Friedman), was formed largely on the strength of its stable of chat hosts, whom Friedman and his team had identified and cultivated over the past few years.

In addition, the moderator would be responsible for setting policy for the community's approach to editorial control of member-generated content. What will the community not allow to appear? How can it respect both freedom of speech and feelings of members as a whole? Like the secretary of a club, the moderator must set the rules for members and be constantly on the prowl for ideas that might improve the quality of the time members spend with each other. This includes establishing new bulletin boards for members to set up and organizing on-line events. Like special club evenings, these events are occasions when a special guest speaker is invited to join members to give a "talk" on a topic of interest and to respond to questions from the members listening in. ESPNET, the sports site, might announce that an ice hockey goalkeeper will "take questions after practice, Friday, 1.30 P.M. Eastern (U.S.) time."

An effective moderator will turn to the community's hosts and sysops for ideas on how to improve the community's environment for members' interactions. They are closest to the pulse of the community's participants and will have a good sense of when a particular bulletin board or chat area is ripe for splitting into subcommunities—or for weeding out. The community's organic growth will be heavily influenced by these hosts and sysops, and the moderator must decide how best to motivate and compensate these individuals—possibly by creating "franchising" opportunities, as described earlier in the chapter.

Archivist. There is as yet no working model for the role of archivist, whose job it would be to build up the library of member-generated content—an important resource for keeping members interested and informed over time and one of the community's chief sources of long-term distinctiveness. The archivist will develop a process for reviewing the output of the community's bulletin boards and chat areas, deciding what to weed out and what to keep. For example, ESPNET offers "chat transcripts" of conversations that have taken place with celebrity participants, which someone must have recorded, edited, and filed electronically. Such content must be stored in an accessible way, enabling hosts, sysops, and members themselves to draw on it real-time to respond to questions or to feed into conversations. The archivist is not unlike a keeper of sports statistics, who can process vast quantities of information and pass appropriate pieces on to live commentators.

In theory, the archivist will sift through all member-generated content, identifying pieces of interest, marking them, and filing them electronically. In practice, the archivist will have to rely on chat hosts, sysops, and information systems to help perform this role. Hosts should be given guidelines indicating what pieces of content to keep and trained in a system for electronically filing it. Over time, they will develop their own sense of what should be filed. The archivist must also index this information and allow it to be accessed easily. Indexing is probably the greatest challenge of all, given that the structure of subcommunities will change as the community evolves, making it difficult for archives to mirror the community's structure exactly. The archivist must be adept at handling information and be current in systems and software technology. Because the role of archivist focuses on member-generated content, it might report to the executive moderator.

Community editor. The community editor is responsible for the community's nonmember content—that is, content published by external companies or created by the community organizer itself. This material might range from on-line magazines and articles to statistics, real-time information services, and searchable databases. In a business-to-business community for farmers, for instance, the editor might have to ensure that the community is fed with up-to-date commodity price indices, weather conditions nationwide, articles on foodstuffs or fertilizers, and newsletters on legal issues or current lobbying campaigns to legislative bodies. The editor would *not* be responsible for the advertising of used farm equipment on bulletin boards or for discussions of the latest politicking in chat areas and on-line forums; these would count as member-generated content.

The term *editor* is, like sysop or chat host, widely used. For example, at Total New York, a site mentioned in chapter 5, there is a position titled editor and programming director. It is the editor's responsibility to understand members' needs for information and to match these needs up with the relevant sources of information. The editor might negotiate with external providers of such content and create value for members by balancing price, convenience, and quality. Alternatively, since all communities will generate at least some of their own "published" content, the editor would oversee its creation by a team of content developers. Larger communities will start to create such published content as in-house electronic magazines or databases that leverage user-generated content. The editor should be responsible for deciding what types of this editorial content the community should develop itself and what it should source externally.

Customer service manager. Responding to participants' questions quickly and simply is strategically important if first-time visitors are to feel welcomed into the community and to develop into full-fledged members. This is all about casework, and it will be tough to execute because of the likely variety in types of calls the customer service desk will receive. Some will be from computer beginners who are still trying to figure out how to move off the home page into the community. Others will be to alert the community that its server is down. Still others will be totally unrelated to the community ("Why was my Internet access bill so high last month?"). The customer service manager's job is to make sure that all of these calls are handled effectively without incurring enormous expense.

Given the cost of labor, customer service can be a major expense in a community's early years. The community can certainly try to off-load (or claim a refund for) customer service calls relating directly and exclusively to transactions being conducted with a community vendor— although a community will probably view the quality of its customer service as a factor that differentiates it from its competitors and so may absorb even these costs itself.

Member satisfaction will be the key measure of success for this function, and the community's bulletin boards will probably be a direct source of feedback on how the function can improve. Given that this is a major cost center, that many calls are likely to be similar, and that there is the need for twenty-four-hour coverage, this is very likely to be a function that is shared across the entire community, or across communities in the case of constellations and coalitions.

Information systems manager. Information systems managers will clearly have a pivotal, behind-the-scenes role in managing the community. They must ensure that the community has adequate server capacity to store all the community's content—its member-generated and published material—and to archive its member profiles. They must also ensure that the community has adequate transmission capacity—the phone lines that link community members' calls into and between the community's servers. Like customer service, "feedback" will come in only when things go wrong. At a more strategic level, these managers must ensure the security of all financial data flows in and out of the community. They must work with the archivist to design the system that allows access to archived member-generated content. They must also develop a system that not only stores member profiles and guarantees member privacy but also produces routine and customized reports that serve the needs of the community's managers as well as its vendors and advertisers.

Given the enormous quantities of data to be handled, and the resulting technical complexity, it is likely that this position will require a level of expertise that few communities will be able to afford for themselves. Communities are therefore likely either to share this function with other communities or, more probably, to outsource it. It is a safe bet that many large corporations such as IBM and AT&T will offer such services to community organizers.

Community developer. Like real estate developers, community developers are project managers, responsible for establishing new subcommunities or services. They are not the only ones responsible for the community's innovation. (If innovation is not widely understood to be the community's lifeblood, the pace of member acquisition will slow and membership will slowly erode.) The developer's role is to work with hosts, sysops, editors, and members (among others) to understand what subcommunities need to be seeded and fed and then to get it done. This may be another of those roles that only larger communities can afford; smaller communities may expect people in other positions, such as host, to perform this function.

Community architect. The community architect optimizes a community's structure and design. This role is filled today by software developers and Internet consultants. While a community developer is focused on managing the creation of new subcommunities, a community architect might be retained to advise on issues that are either specific, such as working with sysops on the design of individual bulletin boards, or more general, such as the overall structure of a community. For example, the community developer in a travel community might focus on setting up dozens of new subcommunities to serve emerging member needs in a wide variety of geographical areas—including Paris, London, Venice, Fiji, Hawaii—and might create a high degree of complexity in the process. A community architect will help determine how to balance the desire to meet members' needs and be innovative with the need to make sure each chat area and bulletin board has a critical mass of member interest. In this case, the architect might suggest creating a subcommunity for the Pacific Islands before creating separate areas for Fiji and Hawaii. In addition, a community architect might be retained to work with the editor and content developers on how to improve the community's user interface and menu structure (the sequence of steps a member takes to reach a desired destination) or on how to balance the community's ratio of published versus member-generated content.

It is clearly not essential for every community to have its own architect. This position is likely to be shared across communities or outsourced, but if it exists within a community, it might be filled or overseen by a manager of community development, who would also be responsible for the community's developers.

Value extraction

As a community focuses on extracting value by building up its level of advertising and transaction revenues, it will place increasing emphasis on two roles: information analyst and community merchandiser.

Information analyst. Information analysts are likely to be the unsung hero(ine)s of many communities. They will be responsible for managing member profiles, the vast quantities of data generated by the recording of a participant's clicks on the keyboard while inside the community's electronic boundaries. They must analyze members' patterns of behavior and deduce from these digital footprints what is important to members and what is not, what can be improved, and how. They must also assess the performance of vendors in terms of the transaction volume they are stimulating and content publishers in terms of the member usage they are attracting. This is not an executive role but an advisory one. In practice it will involve producing tracking reports that provide managers with regular feedback. This would include, for example, information on participants' demographics and their behavioral trends within the community: how many people have visited each bulletin board, how many logged questions and how many provided answers, how much time was spent in each chat area, how many participated in on-line forums, how many and who bought how much from which vendors.

There will be at least five applications of this information:

1. To enhance the community's existing offers, including the type and depth of content, the community's design and layout, the range of vendors and content publishers represented, and possibly even the range and characteristics of the products they offer.

2. To drive structural decisions being made by the community's executive producer, architect, developer, and hosts. Usage patterns should indicate which bulletin boards and chat areas are most frequently visited and therefore which areas of the broader community may be ripe for fractal division into subcommunities.

3. To recruit new members. The data should allow the community organizer to understand the characteristics of different types of members and therefore to target individuals with similar profiles.

4. To generate advertising and transaction revenues. Packaged in summary form, the data should demonstrate the attractiveness of the community's membership to vendors. On receiving members' approval, the information can be shared with advertisers to indicate which members might be interested in receiving targeted product information or an order form. This should in the long term be an

efficient way for vendors to reach target audiences as communities achieve a critical mass of members. Unfortunately, some vendors are taking a short-term view of efficiency and using mass e-mailing services to unload a cheap deluge of e-mails indiscriminately into on-line users' e-mailboxes. This could trigger a backlash against on-line marketing in general.

5. To help vendors understand their products' strengths and weaknesses, as perceived by community members. As we will discuss in chapter 9, virtual communities can be an effective tool for generating direct feedback on products.

Part of the analyst's function—the storage and mechanical processing of the data and its synthesis into report form—might be outsourced. But at a minimum the analyst must define the requirements for the information architecture: what information should be captured, in what format, and how it should be stored. A good analyst will also be able to spot implications from consistent patterns observed in member profiles (such as the frequency of visits to certain vendors or parts of the community) and to develop recommendations for managers to act on (such as making it easier to reach a certain part of the community) that serve the interests of the community's members as well as its vendors. A community's ability to absorb and respond to its members' behavior is what will create competitive advantage for the community.

Community merchandiser. The community merchandiser is responsible for meeting the transactional needs of the community's members by ensuring that the providers of goods and services desired by members are encouraged to participate in the community. The merchandiser is also responsible for maximizing the community's revenues from advertising and transactions, which is one indicator that the first function is being performed effectively.

Two roles the organizer can't do without: information analysts and community merchandisers.

"Meeting the transactional needs" of the community means first finding out what products community members want to learn about or buy on-line. Reports from the information analyst should help. The merchandiser should also be helped by information gleaned by chat hosts and sysops from members' comments in chat areas and on bulletin boards. Hosts might even ask members about their preferences directly. The merchandiser is then responsible for recruiting the vendors of interest to members and for mining member profiles for information about the community to make it an attractive marketplace for those vendors.

There are several ways the merchandiser can "maximize advertising and transaction revenues." First, assuming the community organizer receives a percentage commission on transactions conducted within the community, it is the merchandiser's role to set the "right" commission. At this level, the community maximizes its revenues by striking a balance between keeping commissions high enough to be significant yet low enough to make it worthwhile for vendors to market actively to members. In addition to setting commission levels, some merchandisers might try to increase revenues by actively selling goods and services on-line. Like a TV shopping channel, the community could use one or two highly effective merchandisers to drum up sales across the entire community. Doing this, though, might damage the community organizer's role as a trusted and objective third party.

On the advertising side, a merchandiser could stimulate revenues by achieving high success rates for advertisers. This means helping vendors to direct their advertising to those members most likely to want to see it. This could be done by using relatively straightforward information from member profiles (such as which bulletin boards a member has participated in). So members posting messages on bulletin boards focused on travel to Italy, for example, might automatically receive e-mail messages on special fares from Alitalia. In addition, to improve advertising effectiveness and so command higher revenues, the merchandiser might help advertisers tailor their message, again based on the analyst's information. So if certain segments of a travel community appear to value price over service and prefer the convenience of bundling all elements of a vacation together, the merchandiser might advise Alitalia to develop advertising for these members that stresses low prices and offers complete Italian vacation packages. While straightforward conceptually, this would be hard to accomplish. It would demand a high degree of attention on the part of hosts or the capture of information at a more detailed level than who has visited which bulletin boards. It would also require considerable flexibility on the part of vendors.

The merchandiser is responsible for ensuring that commerce can take place efficiently and securely within the community. This includes arranging for secure payment systems. He or she must also identify ways in which to facilitate commercial transactions between community members. This might involve establishing a "classified ad" section or developing a more sophisticated set of transaction services, especially in business-to-business communities. For example, private "meeting rooms" could be set up for brokers to interact confidentially with buyers and sellers, and a full slate of support services could be offered, including credit checks, testing services, and access to legal or tariff information.

Finally, the merchandiser performs a crucial role by balancing the sometimes conflicting needs of vendors and members. Vendors may want to bombard members with e-mails advertising their products or specific promotions; some already are today. Some members will want to receive these messages; others will definitely not. The merchandiser must work with both parties to establish a happy medium. The catch-word should always be "community before commerce."

MANAGEMENT REQUIREMENTS

Listing the requirements for growth and skills is one thing; putting them into action in the virtual community is another. It will be management's job to fill the roles we have described and to orchestrate the coming together of policies and people around common goals.

Source and develop skills effectively

Finding people to fill the positions discussed in this chapter will not be a simple task, even assuming a community can afford them. Some functions exist already in the on-line world, others have yet to emerge but have analogs in other industries, and the remainder as yet do not exist anywhere.

Functions that are already emerging in some numbers in the on-line world include the sysop, chat host, on-line editor, customer service manager, and information systems manager. For example, there are some 40,000 sysops in the United States alone, many of them running their own independent bulletin board services (BBSs). There are thousands of chat hosts—though these vary widely in quality. There are also hundreds of on-line editors serving in the large on-line services (such as AOL, CompuServe, Prodigy, and the Microsoft Network), as well as many more in recent on-line start-ups. Customer service is well developed at these same services, as is information systems management.

Harder functions to fill are those that have yet to emerge but which have analogs in other industries. These include merchandisers, marketers, and information analysts. Merchandising is clearly an important function in many industries. While the closest parallels are probably to be found in TV home-shopping companies, the required skills may also be adaptable from the shopping mall and department store industries, where managers must attract retailers to sell in their mall or store as well as understand local customers' needs. Information analysts, too, have yet to emerge in significant numbers in the on-line arena. There are, however, close parallels at companies that manage large amounts of data for customers, such as Nielsen and IRI, which track the purchases of shoppers at food stores around the United States, and at the companies Nielsen and IRI serve, which often have sophisticated research departments.

Functions that have yet to emerge anywhere include archivists, community developers, and community architects. Leaving aside keepers of sports statistics, archivists may have to be developed from among the hosts and sysops who have both the in-depth knowledge of the community and the gut instincts to know what material is likely to be of lasting interest. Successful organizers of small subcommunities might be groomed to become community developers or architects.

Four roles stand out in their importance to a community's long-term value: the *marketers* who interest people in a community and build membership; the *hosts and sysops* who create a stimulating environment that makes people want to return to the community and become involved; the *merchandisers* who are able to recruit appropriate vendors and advertisers and help them adapt to this new selling environment; and the *usage analysts* who successfully gather and interpret information and develop member and vendor profiles that are of value to moderators, editors, marketers, vendors, advertisers, and, most important, members. Given the lead times involved in developing these skills, the community organizer should start building them as soon as the community's economics allow.

Set appropriate performance metrics

Drawing a community's roles on an organization chart is one thing; making them work in practice is another. Once in the organization, the various functions may have conflicting interests and priorities. Some of these conflicts may sound familiar: where an editor might want to see some space on a page left open to enhance its look, the merchandiser might see a unique placement opportunity for an advertisement. Where hosts and sysops might see a need to respond to members' interests by setting up dozens of new subcommunities, the architect might see a need to minimize complexity by keeping the number of new subcommunities low. Setting the right performance metrics will have two mutually reinforcing effects. They will act as a focusing device for the organization, balancing conflicting needs, and they will act as an integrating device across functions and skill sets, harnessing them to a set of common tasks or processes. Editors and merchandisers might be unified around a goal of maximizing membership. Since life is never that simple, they will also have to ensure that the community is meeting its financial targets. In fact, one of the key roles performance metrics will generally play is to balance respon-

Organic management without the right performance metrics is unlikely to create lasting value.

siveness to members' needs with the community's own long-term economic health. If organic growth is to be economically healthy, not out of control, it must be carefully tended and directed.

The executive producer, whose role it is to guide the community up the growth curve, should set performance metrics for the management group that reflect the community's next strategic objective. So in the early stages, when the focus is on achieving critical mass of members, the management group should be unified on such points as the number of members to be acquired and low churn rates, but it should also be in agreement on keeping the cost of acquiring members low. As the emphasis shifts toward increasing the level of usage and acquiring vendors and advertisers, the average usage time and transaction commissions generated on-line will take on more importance than new member acquisition. However, the team should always remember the principle of "community before commerce" to keep the organization's eye on what matters most—the members' interests and their relationships with one another.

8

equipping the
community

choosing the right technology

Don't be seduced or scared off by the
dazzling range of technological options
out there. Virtual communities are
not about using the best or most powerful
technologies. In fact, you may want
to avoid the most innovative technology
wherever possible, the better to maintain
leverage and speed. Bet on the Internet
long term, but in the meantime seek out
and acquire the technologies you'll need
to start building a commercially successful
virtual community.

IN OUR EXPERIENCE, THE NUMBER ONE THING that keeps the senior management of large companies from launching a virtual community is discomfort with the technology choices required to be successful. (The entrepreneurs we've run across tend to be a bit more comfortable with this issue.) At one level this discomfort is understandable. It's all too easy, on venturing into cyberspace, to become seduced or overwhelmed by the multitude of technological options available.

Yet it's quite possible to overcome this discomfort by staying focused on member needs and by adhering closely to the principles of speed and leverage. With few exceptions, technology is not likely to be the most important factor in determining the commercial success of a virtual community. It is, in fact, a relatively small part of the total investment and operating cost. Early experiences on the network suggest that the key technologies required to address the four broad interaction needs of fantasy, interest, relationship, and transaction are already in place. Technology innovation is rapidly addressing unresolved issues such as security and the need for

Technology isn't the most important factor in virtual communities. Members are.

metering software that measures who did what where on the network, a prerequisite for developing the member profiles that advertisers and vendors will need to target potential audience and customers more precisely. Meanwhile, hosting services offered by companies like America Online, AT&T, and IBM are emerging to provide turnkey network and computing platforms for nontechnology companies that want to operate virtual communities on the network but don't want to invest heavily in technology or the development of the expertise required to deploy and operate it.

A far greater risk is that management will overinvest in leading-edge technology in an effort to create differentiation. Not only does such overinvestment add financial risk, but it also increases operational risk and the potential lead times required to deliver key services. Remember: Success in the virtual community business hinges not on technology-driven differentiation but on strategies designed to accelerate member acquisition and to create deep understanding of the needs of those members.

PRINCIPLES UNDERLYING A TECHNOLOGY STRATEGY

With all of the above now said, it is of course necessary to have a technology strategy in place. The most effective strategies will be based on the dual concepts of speed and leverage. The following seven guidelines will help flesh out what such a strategy might look like.

1. Use proven technologies wherever possible—maintain a strong bias for proven technologies that have already emerged as de facto or de jure standards.

2. Avoid technology innovation at the customer interface and instead concentrate on incorporating the most robust technology for information capture and analysis. This will help accelerate your drive to exploit the commercial potential of virtual communities.

3. Be disciplined and creative in defining member environments and services that can be delivered with existing technologies. For example, some forms of advertising—brand image creation for some consumer goods, for instance—typically require video to be effective. Currently, video cannot be conveniently and cost effectively delivered in the on-line medium. Options for community organizers are either to focus in the near term on forms of advertising that do not require video or to "reinvent" a form of advertising that can be delivered over existing on-line media. (Examples are the early initiatives on the Mama Ragu and Zima Web sites.)

4. Avoid developing any technology in-house.

5. Carefully evaluate the evolving competition among technology providers when sourcing technologies that have not yet emerged as broad-based standards. Both Microsoft and Netscape are engaged in a fierce battle to define the broader technology architecture that will allow electronic commerce to flourish on the Internet. Both are trying to mobilize a broader "web" of technology providers to supply key components of these new architectures and to create the sense of momentum necessary to persuade others to adopt these architectures. (When we refer to technology webs, we do not mean the World Wide Web but an important new form of competition between clusters of technology companies promoting a specific architecture or vision of how various technology components should relate to each other. These companies have few if any formal relationships with each other but are united by their commitment to a specific set of standards that define a distinctive architecture.) Monitor this battle and the shifting alliances and investments among a broader range of providers jockeying for position within one of these technology webs. Be particularly careful about sourcing technology linked to a technology web that appears to be losing momentum in the marketplace—or that perhaps never gained the momentum to begin with. Even if it appears to be a superior technology, it may not turn out to be the standard.

Choose technology for speed and leverage.

6. Design a modular technology architecture. This will allow you to "swap out" key technology components if they begin to lose ground in the marketplace in terms of price or performance and to replace them with new components as they become available.

7. Carefully develop information architectures at the outset to help focus sourcing of appropriate data capture, storage, and manipulation technologies. The challenge will be to anticipate information categories that will be most relevant over time in three areas: member-generated information, member usage and transaction profiles, and economic information (churn rates, cost per member acquisition, cash generation versus cash consumption in the virtual community by member/service segment). Will the information

architecture enable the community organizer to capture and access the most relevant information about the community and its members? Specifically, how detailed is the profile of the community members that can be accumulated over time? Does it provide a rich view of transaction histories and the areas where community members spend their time?

SELECTING THE RIGHT NETWORK PLATFORM

One of the key issues confronting community organizers will be the near-term choice of whether to participate in an on-line service like America Online or to venture immediately onto the Internet, even though the Internet may as yet lack a fully developed infrastructure for commercial transactions. This choice is an important one. A wrong choice could result in significant delays when the organizer has to shift to an alternative network platform and/or in the loss of profitability potential. At the extreme, it may mean the difference between success or failure.

Unfortunately, this choice is complicated by a zealous debate between partisans of the two platform types. Advocates of the Internet argue that the standards established around basic communication protocols (TCP/IP) and text description languages (HTML) offer more opportunity for growth and innovation than proprietary technology platforms. They cite the massive shift that occurred in the computer business during the 1980s from proprietary mainframe and minicomputer architectures to the open architectures that developed around the de facto standards defined by Intel and Microsoft in PCs.

Those who favor on-line services reply that technology standards need to be robust and responsive to user needs. Arguing that such standards have yet to emerge to accommodate commercial activity on the Internet, they champion nonstandard technology platforms that can meet the demand for such activity now, not at some indefinite time in the future.

The debate over business models

But technology is only part of the equation. At a deeper level, the heated debate between partisans of the Internet and champions of proprietary on-line services is really about business models. There is a far more important question to be answered than which technology will win, namely: which of the competing business models represented by these networks will prove most successful at creating economic value for participants?

Proponents of the Internet argue that its strength lies in its enormous diversity of resources—far greater than any business could hope to assemble in one place. They claim that users will be comfortable using navigation tools and specialized services (including directories like Yahoo! and search engines like Infoseek) to locate and access resources from a plethora of independent suppliers.

Proponents of on-line services respond that while "surfing" may suit technologically literate users, the mass market will never be lured onto such a dispersed network. They insist that most people will want one-stop shopping—bundled services that assemble, organize, and merchandise a broad range of resources. While they concede that some surfing may occur, they believe users will tend to "settle" into familiar areas of the network that effectively address their needs.

Ultimately, viewing the Internet and proprietary networks as opposing forces in a battle may force an unrealistic either/or choice between them. Hybrid solutions will emerge that meet the needs of businesses and users better than either option alone.

If resource aggregation by virtual community organizers is the most attractive business model, the debate surrounding the choice of network platform becomes more clear-cut. It is a matter of evaluating the technologies required to build virtual community businesses and assessing how long it might take to achieve the specific functionality necessary to support the business model. For example, when will the Internet develop a standardized approach to tracking the activities of individuals across multiple Web sites (which must take place before targeted advertising programs can be unleashed)? When will a widely accepted approach to authentication—verifying that a person is in fact who they say they are—emerge (which will be essential to driving the growth of commercial transactions)?

Foundation and overlay technology choices

How community organizers approach the selection of a platform depends partly on what other organizers (and businesses in general) choose to do. If several major players select the Internet as their primary network, for instance, their choice will probably accelerate the development of commerce-related technologies on this platform, making it even more attractive to later entrants.

Part of the technology debate seems to be over already. De facto standards have clearly emerged around such basic technologies as the method for connecting diverse networks (TCP/IP protocols). Most players recognize that these standard foundation technologies offer far more flexibility at lower cost than comparable nonstandard options offered originally by on-line services and specialized private networks. After initially pursuing a nonstandard strategy, late entrants into the on-line services business such as Microsoft and AT&T have now made a U-turn and endorsed standards. Similarly, Prodigy and Compuserve are currently migrating to a completely standard set of foundation technologies, while America Online is shifting its core network platform to a TCP/IP foundation.

More problematic are the additional overlays of technology needed to conduct commercial activities and to give users the richer experiences of 3-D graphics, animation, video, and sound. Several technologies are involved:

- *Transactions and payment technologies:* Vendors usually prefer to get paid for their offerings, and community members will want to know that a broadly used payment system is available, a system that can verify the identity of the business asking for payment and make sure their payments are secure. Payment technologies will need to be able to handle both large and small (less than $10) payments.

- *Metering and data collection software:* To reimburse publishers for their content, community organizers must be able to identify which members access their community, what content areas they visit, how much time they spend there, and what transactions they conduct. Technologies that supply this information will be vital in billing members, in attracting advertisers eager to know who the audience is and what members do while visiting the community, and in attracting vendors eager to target members with the right kind of transaction profile.

- *Integration technologies:* One of the hallmarks of multimedia-enabled networks is their ability to combine content and communication. Yet the Internet evolved as a highly segmented network, with one area delivering published content (the World Wide Web), another providing bulletin board services (USENET news groups), and a third offering real-time chat (Internet Relay Chat). Virtual communities will be better able to leverage the Internet's capabilities once there is technology in place that integrates these three services so that members enjoy a more seamless experience.

- *Graphics and animation software:* The race is on to deliver ever more compelling visuals, but the technologies (including compression) required to create 3-D graphics and moving images are far from standardized. This creates a major problem for network users and for content developers. The former will have to install multiple versions of software to access graphics-intensive sites, while the latter will have to learn to work with multiple graphics and animation software packages or risk becoming tied to one that fails to become a standard.

- *"Streaming" content delivery:* Voice, sound, and video delivery depend on the delivery of real-time "streams" to the network user despite bandwidth and traffic constraints. Such constraints are a particular problem in router-based networks like the Internet, which do not establish dedicated circuits between content provider and network user but instead have to contend with uncertain and often complicated router paths, not to mention other traffic being sent over the same lines.

Difficult choices

The overlay technologies just discussed are far more fully developed and standardized in proprietary on-line platforms (such as AOL's), which presents a dilemma for organizers seeking to establish virtual communities on the Internet. Should they sign up with one of the proprietary on-line services to make sure they get the overlay technologies they need to build their virtual community? Or should they venture out on the Internet, where these technologies, let alone the standards for them, are not yet defined?

If they opt for the Internet, they must consider how they will compete with communities residing on proprietary on-line services that are more adept at both deploying technology and acquiring members. On the other hand, making the decision to go to an on-line service using proprietary technologies has a number of drawbacks: the technology may be abandoned, the on-line service may develop the primary relationship with members, and the on-line service will extract its share of the value created by community organizers—and may possibly take an increasing share as they become locked in to nonstandard technologies.

Faced with these prospects, aspiring community organizers may well decide to hedge their bets by residing on the Internet (to maintain their independence) but also by using nonstandard overlay technologies to overcome limitations on functionality relative to the on-line services. These nonstandard overlay technologies would include products in the categories outlined above: transactions and payments technologies; metering and data collection software; integration technologies; graphics and animation software; and technologies able to "stream" voice, sound, and video.

The need to accelerate entry. The advantages of being a first-mover and the urgency these advantages communicate will motivate Internet-based organizers to jump-start the technology adoption process. Rather than waiting for competing technologies to settle down around de facto standards, virtual community organizers are likely to opt for speed and deploy nonstandard technologies to build their businesses.

The urge to move now may be reinforced by the emerging "hosting" businesses on the Internet. These businesses are already assembling platforms that combine standard foundation technologies with nonstandard overlays to supply the complete functionality virtual communities need. Community organizers finding it difficult or risky to evaluate competing technologies and to cobble together their own nonstandard overlays will value the guarantee provided by a host that can deliver a functioning commercial platform tailored to their specific needs.

In evaluating these services, beyond evaluating the functionality and cost of the existing hosting platform, community organizers need to focus on a broader question. What is the relationship between the technology architecture developed by the host and the various technology "webs" emerging on networks? If the host appears to be closely linked to one of the existing technology "webs" (Microsoft or Netscape, for example), the organizer should develop an independent perspective on the likely success of that web versus competing webs on the network. This issue may be somewhat mitigated by the deployment of technology architecture that is sufficiently modular and flexible.

The wait for de facto standards. The trend toward nonstandard technology overlays on the Internet could, of course, be reversed by the rapid emergence of de facto standards for these technologies. Certainly, strong incentives will exist for content providers and network users to push for standards definition. The former will incur extra expense if they have to adapt their content to multiple nonstandard technology platforms, while the latter will have to suffer the inconvenience of incompatibilities within the network. Early success in the area of macropayment systems, where Visa and MasterCard are cooperating to define a common set of standards, provides grounds for optimism.

The good news is that investment in the key overlay technologies has been substantial, and a range of solutions will be brought to market over the next year or two. The bad news is that there are many solutions, and each of their developers is anxiously seeking a return on investment. Few are likely to support an emerging de facto standard that is not their own.

The probable near-term result is intense competition between technology solutions as developers seek to accelerate adoption, build a broad installed base, and capture value-creation opportunities. Network-based businesses will reinforce this fragmentation as they scramble to implement technologies now rather than wait for standards to emerge.

The best of both worlds. While the eventual outcome is still uncertain, the most likely scenario is the emergence of a hybrid network environment that embraces the best of both Internet and proprietary options.

In the hybrid network scenario, differences between proprietary on-line services and the Internet begin to blur as businesses respond to user needs for bringing resources together into "bundles" that are easier to navigate than a fragmented Internet. On the one hand, the proprietary on-line services continue to migrate to the de facto standard foundation technologies found on the Internet. This allows them to provide their members with enhanced access to the full range of resources available on the Internet while also continuing to provide a unique set of resources available only to their members. They also pay

Expect a hybrid network.

increasing attention to new business models, such as virtual communities. On the other hand, "new game" players begin to emerge on the Internet, deploying nonstandard technology overlays to speed their entry into the virtual community business. This implies a clustering of the Internet, at least in the near term, into "islands" of commercial opportunity.

To fuel commercial growth and respond to consumer needs, all players will probably adopt an opportunistic approach to deploying technology platforms, embracing de facto standards where they exist and relying on nonstandard technology overlays elsewhere. Competition will revolve less around technology platforms than around participants' skill and flexibility in executing a fundamentally new business model. Positioning choices will be driven by a clear understanding of the functionality required to implement the model and by a deep appreciation of the advantages conferred on first-movers.

Other scenarios. While the hybrid between the Internet and proprietary networks is the most likely scenario, it is clearly not the only one. Several others might evolve, these depending on the timing of technology deployment, the choices made by major network-based businesses, and the behavior of users.

- Proprietary on-line services may achieve an invincible lead-time advantage in building businesses like virtual communities, overwhelming players that bravely venture out onto the Internet. This scenario will be especially likely if there are delays in the deployment of overlay technologies on the Internet or if some of the early implementations "blow up"—if there were, say, a massive breach in payment security.

- De facto standards may quickly emerge for overlay technologies on the Internet, preserving the value of a homogeneous platform. Virtual communities would then opt for the Internet rather than run the risk of becoming dependent on the proprietary on-line services as intermediaries between themselves and their users. Successful virtual communities that are already lodged in proprietary environments, such as Motley Fool on America Online, would migrate to the more widely accessible Internet platform. Over time, this migration could relegate the proprietary on-line services to a much more limited role as access vendors.

- Robust agent and filtering technology, combined with growing user sophistication, could produce a very different outcome. Examples of such technologies might be agent and filtering software that allow users to predetermine what e-mail or information they want to receive and then block out the rest. With these technologies, individual network users might take over some functions of the virtual community, such as customizing content and communication services to suit their needs. Vendors would thus be less likely to be put in the position of having to use the virtual community as an intermediary between them and their users, but they would still face the threat of more informed customers demanding higher levels of service at lower prices or unleashing their agents to track down more accommodating vendors.

Implications for community organizers

Rather than joining the rather sterile debate that pits the Internet against proprietary on-line services, virtual community organizers should devote their efforts to developing the business model that best meets the needs of network users—especially the vast majority who have yet to venture on-line.

Outcomes are indeed uncertain, but by staying focused on business models and their functionality, virtual community organizers should develop a degree of flexibility and a sense of urgency that will serve them well as they navigate through the confusing and constantly changing seas of technological innovation. Technology is not the object but merely the enabler that facilitates the delivery of value to end users. Clarity about the value that is to be delivered and the timing required for success will act as the compass that helps virtual community organizers stay on course.

Even with this compass, the direction in which community organizers should head in the near term is not clear. Urgency suggests building communities on proprietary on-line services where the necessary technologies are available today. Leverage argues against locking into proprietary technology environments relative to the Internet. The Internet provides a set of open standards that encourages a diverse range of companies to invest in creating and delivering a broad range of innovative technologies that "plug in" to the basic Internet platform. As a result, innovative approaches to such diverse areas as 3-D graphics, streaming audio, and encryption are being developed and deployed on a daily basis. In contrast, the company owning a proprietary on-line service platform bears most of the burden for investing in technology innovation. Not only does that generally mean less money will be available overall for investment in technology innovation (even a very large company cannot afford to invest amounts equivalent to hundreds of companies on an open platform), it also limits the potential for innovation (one company typically cannot match the scope of innovation represented by hundreds of independent companies, each with their own unique perspective on how to tackle a particular need). The open architecture of the personal computer opened up a torrent of innovation relative to the proprietary architectures of the mainframe and even the minicomputer. In a similar way, the open architecture of the Internet is likely to bring about more innovation over time than any proprietary network platform.

This conflict cannot be easily resolved. Two paths are possible. Consider setting up a community initially on a proprietary on-line service to take advantage of the early learning and the opportunity to get a head start in acquiring a critical mass of members. If you choose this path, consider developing a parallel site for your community on the Internet. This is the option pursued by Motley Fool and SeniorNet. Use the community on the on-line service platform as a channel for funneling members over time to your Internet location. This will reduce the risk of suffering the longer-term profit squeeze that may result from excessive dependence on the on-line service for nonstandard technology sourcing and member acquisition and management.

The other option is to move immediately to the Internet and modify the sophistication and range of services supplied to the community as the technology becomes available. This is the option chosen by such Internet start-ups as the Main Quad, an emerging virtual community targeting college students, and Talk City, an emerging collection of virtual communities relying heavily on Internet Relay Chat for chat capability. These start-ups must wrestle with which nonstandard technology overlays to deploy (such as Well Engaged, a software product strengthening member communication on the Web) and how to reduce the risk of being caught with a technology that falls behind if competing technologies win the standards race.

As we conclude this second part of the book, it may be a good time to admit that while we did not set out to write a "how-to" guide to virtual communities, we're mindful that some readers may be interested in exploring the questions of which issues and tasks they should address first as they start building a community. To that end we've put together a "Management Agenda" that appears at the end of the book. This agenda points managers toward specific tasks that will help them get started in organizing a virtual community.

III

positioning to win the
broader game

9

rethinking functional management

Virtual communities are not just a stand-alone business opportunity that companies can take or leave as they wish. By shifting power generally from the vendor to the customer, virtual communities will irrevocably alter the way large companies market and sell to customers in their core businesses. These changes will demand new ways of thinking about and approaching the marketing and sales functions.

AS VIRTUAL COMMUNITIES TIP THE BALANCE of power in commercial transactions toward the customer, they'll provide a powerful vehicle for vendors to deepen and broaden their relationships with customers. This is likely to affect the way traditional businesses are run in "physical space" as well as in the virtual world. The primary effects will be felt by managers in the marketing and sales functions (see figure 9-1), who will find themselves wrestling with new rules for winning customer loyalty. In fact, "ownership" of customer relationships as a whole is likely to be thrown up for grabs by the emergence of virtual communities. These threats to the status quo will also represent opportunities. Marketers stand to gain, on balance, from the implications of virtual communities (see figure 9-2), especially those who find ways to leverage this new customer power rather than fight it.

MARKETING AND SELLING TO MORE POWERFUL CUSTOMERS

Earlier in the book we discussed how virtual communities are likely to shift power from vendor to customer by reducing or eliminating the information advantages that vendors currently enjoy. This is not all bad news for marketers. Because virtual communities will actually improve the quality of information about individual customers and give customers a reason for releasing that information to vendors, virtual communities will allow innovative marketers to move closer to treating customers as "segments of one." Virtual communities will also allow marketers to leverage customers' ideas in designing and commercializing products and to leverage customers' voices in promoting them.

Communities will undoubtedly create challenges as well. In this on-line environment, marketers must rely more on the quality of their product than on the strength of their brand; they must learn how to make advertising sell, not just communicate; and they must adjust their pricing strategies to survive in a world of more efficient markets. Successful marketers could end up enjoying a kind of customer loyalty that they can now only imagine. As a result, sales forces will be able to

Figure 9-1 The Impact of the Virtual Community on Traditional Business Functions

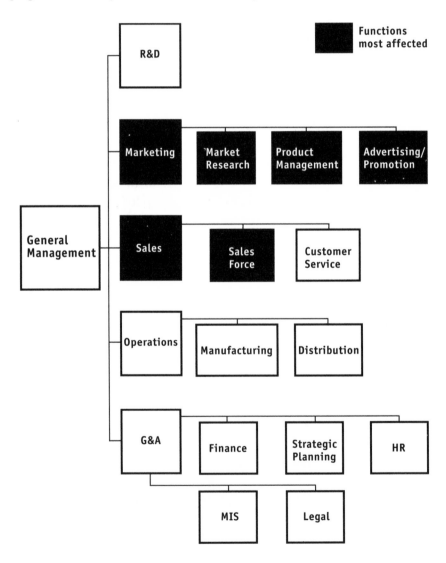

focus less on "selling" to customers and more on "managing" and "serving" them.

Market to "segments of one"

Marketers long ago mastered the art of mass marketing. But the next frontier—"mass customization"—has proven more difficult to achieve. The concept has intensified marketers' focus on the objective of identifying, and building relationships with, a company's current and potential best customers, with the financial goal of having them concentrate a disproportionately high share of their value with that company. An essential factor in meeting this objective is the selection, communication, and delivery of a product value proposition that is tailored to stimulate the most profitable types of transactions with the individual customer. Virtual communities are the mechanism that can bring this vision of relationship-based, individually tailored marketing to reality.

Essential to this effort will be the new sources of customer information virtual communities can provide. If communities are successful—as measured in terms of numbers of participants, amount of time spent in the community, and transaction intensity—the profiles they create on individual customers will yield rich data sets about both individuals and customer segments. These data sets will create detailed transaction histories, at the level of the individual customer, that can be used to predict future opportunities to transact with a given customer. (Firefly, an on-line agent software put out by Agents, Inc., does this

Figure 9-2 Potential Implications of Communities for Marketers

- Reduce emphasis on value of vendor's branding
- Facilitate price comparisons
- Allow comments to be made on product/service in public, not in confidence
- Increase volume of information to be analyzed
- Change the rules of advertising/promotion

- Expand demand for product/service
- Increase word-of-mouth promotion of product/service
- Stimulate customer feedback
- Generate richer information on customers, markets
- Eliminate separation of advertising and transactions
- Allow advertising to be seen as helpful, not intrusive

today in the field of consumer entertainment products. It allows users to create profiles of their music and movie preferences and allows vendors to use this information to sell products to them one-on-one based on their past preferences.) The data might also be used by vendors—if community members approve—to identify which current and *potential* customers are more valuable than others. This applies particularly to the world of coalitions described in chapter 4; coalition organizers have access to data that cut across communities and therefore to a more complete picture of customers' transaction histories.

One effect of this new customer information will be to make the market researcher's life harder. If the market researcher's job today is difficult enough in terms of effectively managing disparate data to enable senior executives to make decisions, it will become exponentially more complex. First, the market researcher must relearn what is doable and what is not in terms of obtaining customer information. There are many mechanisms for capturing information on-line, and they vary in scope and accuracy. Asking users to register at a site, for example, will not by itself help the market researcher track their activity within the site. (Even registration is complicated because there are several ways to register on-line users.)

The researcher must understand which vendors have rights to what data, how to respect customer privacy, and where to go for customer data. In some circumstances, community organizers will control customer profiles on members' behalf. In others, this role will be held by the coalition organizer. At the extreme end of the "reverse market," the model changes completely and the individual customer advertises his or her needs rather than releasing profile information. This happens every time a customer sets agent software to work to look for a particular product. In this case, the market researcher's role changes profoundly, helping the customer service function to anticipate these product requests.

Don't let yourself sink under the weight of unused data.

To avoid the problem of sinking under the weight of unused data, the market researcher must establish which data on community participants will be the most useful. In some businesses, complete transaction data are simply not available at the level of the individual customer. In this case, communities will plug an important hole in managers' tool kits. In other businesses, more data is collected on customers than organizations know what to do with. Large stacks of information go unread on managers' desks.

In the on-line world, the market researcher must fall somewhere in the middle, taking advantage of the depth of information available through communities while at the same time bringing focus to the process of data collection and analysis. On-line, a plethora of data can be gathered on users' demographics; the sites they have visited; the ads they have clicked on; and, in some cases, every keystroke they have typed (on-line, that is). Marketers must work with researchers to identify the important questions that a community can uniquely answer. (For example, what events or changes in product features trigger certain types of purchases? What products are traded off against one another before a purchase decision is reached?) They must then focus market research efforts on gathering and interpreting that information. If successful, the marketer will gain an advantage in its on-line markets that can be applied in its off-line markets as well.

Strengthen product strategy

The information generated by members in a community also has value in the form of feedback on the quality of existing products and features. One specialized software developer purchases software packages from a global software supplier and tailors them to the needs of customers in the financial services industry. This developer found that it was not getting adequately responsive service from its supplier. As a result, it helped form something like a small on-line vertical business community on CompuServe that brought together other customers of the same large software supplier. Whenever the software developers had questions, they would post them on the community's bulletin board. They found that they were able to give each other more timely and more effective support than they had previously received from the supplier. Taking this a step further, they started collecting feedback on the products they were purchasing and offered this feedback to the software supplier. To its credit, rather than taking a defensive posture, the supplier adopted many of their recommendations in subsequent versions of the product.

People frequently talk on-line about products, ranging from golf clubs and restaurants to legal services. This happens whether companies want it to or not. In fact, we have seen instances of companies trying to avoid public on-line discussion of their products by curbing the use of their company names and brands in discussion groups—to no avail. Ironically, though their desire to protect trademarks is understandable, the companies concerned are often market leaders who should have the least to fear from discussions among their customers. On this issue, marketers would do well to follow King Canute's example by recognizing the futility of trying to resist the tide and instead seek out ways to harness it to their advantage.

As communities begin to aggregate customers with shared interests and characteristics, they will form live test beds where marketers can reach the most frequent users of their products in a true market environment that focus groups cannot match. Here they can learn directly about improving their products or customers' perception of their products and cull ideas from customers for new product concepts. Since many comments on-line tend to praise products, communities will also emphasize which products or features a marketer should think twice about eliminating. The hallmark of the marketers that "get it" will be their establishment of e-mail links allowing community members to communicate with the company and, better still, bulletin boards and on-line events that facilitate members' communication with each other.

Customer feedback gathered in this way may not be statistically significant in the early years, but it will become so over time as more and more data points are collected. The feedback should generate insights and help target other market research initiatives; it may also point out simple improvements to products or customer service that require no further market research. While this feedback will generally be delivered in public on-line forums where any competitor can also access it, its real value will be released only by those who use it to act on the ideas put forward by customers. Just as in the infomediary world we described in chapter 4, the secret of success will lie not in ownership of information but in its application.

Capitalize on the community's inherent capacity for PR

Communities can be highly effective at stimulating word of mouth. The on-line discussions we just mentioned in connection with strengthening product design can also serve as free PR. As we have mentioned, more often than not people on-line are quick to enthuse about a product's benefits. They allow a company to leverage its most effective sales force: its own customers. Let's look at an example of how this is working in practice. Cobra Golf, Inc., is a golf club manufacturer. The company has created a space on its site for people to post unedited messages on bulletin boards. Sometimes competing products are described on these boards. But read this recent exchange on one of Cobra's own products:

[top] [post reply]
Date: 21.Jun.19— (Fri) -11:53
Author: _____
e-mail: _____@helisys.com
I am looking for a new driver. Currently, I am debating whether to buy the Taylor Made Bubble Titanium driver or the Cobra Ti. Can anyone help me with this situation?

[top] [post reply]
Date: 24.Jun.19__ (Mon)—09:02
Author: ___
eMail: ____.___@aol.com
I recently purchased the 8.5 degree titanium tour driver from Cobra. It is the longest driver I've ever hit. Something to take note of, that isn't advertised by Cobra, is the gear effect of the club. The clubface is rounded such that, should you not hit the sweet spot, the gear effect will bring the ball back into the fairway. I've added 15 yards, at least, to my average drive. Nice shaft and grip, too. FYI I'm a 12 handicap (due to short game and putting difficulties).

The power of this exchange will depend partly on whether the person posting the reply is known and respected by other community members. (In many cases, other bulletin board participants will add comments that corroborate or disagree with prior responses.) But it is sure to carry at least some weight if the nature of the reply convinces other members that the person knows something about golf clubs. To enjoy this type of promotion, marketers must create bulletin boards, just as Cobra Golf has done, take the risk of allowing members to discuss freely both the company's products and those of its competitors, and analyze the results.

Who are you going to trust more—a salesman or your friend?

Rely more on the product than the brand

In interactions like the e-mail exchange we just illustrated, community members focus less on brand (except as a handle for distinguishing products from one another) and more on product features. As community members come to value what other members think of a vendor's products, beyond what the vendor tells them to believe in its advertising, the community begins to take on its own branding power: it begins to assume the "certification" aspects of branding that reassure buyers that their purchase is likely to be one they will be satisfied with.

The community becomes the brand—the product must stand on its own.

The value of the Cobra Golf example lies as much in the fact that the question was asked as in the answer. Someone turned to the on-line community to find out about a specific product. On the one hand, this behavior may seem to undermine the value of a manufacturer's brand: it is no longer sufficient as a token of product quality. On the other hand, this behavior focuses the manufacturer back on the quality of the product itself. On-line, excellence will be rewarded with its own set of profitable dynamics as satisfied customers promote products they are pleased with and in turn lead others to become customers.

Advertise to sell, not just to communicate

Word of mouth is generally accepted as the most effective form of advertising. Given the difficulty of stimulating enough word of mouth to influence mass markets, vendors have turned to advertising to create and sustain a brand's image. If we assert that communities may erode the power of the brand, what role is left for advertising?

Communities will actually increase the role and power of advertising. There will still be value in promoting brands and raising brand awareness. We're not proclaiming the extinction of brands. As long as there are competing products in a marketplace, brands are needed—at a minimum to distinguish similar products from each other in customers' minds. Communities may actually help to build excitement over brands that revolve around image, such as fashionable or high-ticket items. But a far more powerful role will emerge for advertising as the front end of a transaction. On-line, a person can see an advertisement, click on it to obtain more information, and either ask for material to be sent to their e-mail box or, in many cases, order immediately on-line. Add in what's particular to a community—namely, that people (members, sysops, or hosts) are discussing products with each other—and the result is an environment in which the gap between advertising and selling can be minimized and the transition from ad to sale accelerated. Communities should stimulate impulse buying.

This changes the criteria for defining successful advertising. The objective shifts from stimulating recall to keeping the user engaged for long enough to ask for more information or to make a purchase. At the very least, the purpose of the advertisement will be to generate information about potential customers: who they are and how interested they appear to be in the product, based on how deep they go into the site. In high-ticket categories, such as homes, cars, or aircraft engines, the goal will be to establish a dialog with a potential customer rather than to complete a transaction. Alternatively, in keeping with the notion of reverse markets, advertisements might be placed by customers who want to make their needs known to a vendor. Roles are reversed, and customers might now put their needs out to bid.

As the role of advertising changes, its placement and design must change as well. The skills required in on-line advertising will be different from those required in existing media. On-line merchandising should stimulate a purchase right there and then. It will make use of the interactive nature of the technology to make itself exciting to the viewer. It must offer relevant information quickly ("within three clicks" is the rule) and make on-line ordering easy. Thoughtlessly digitizing an existing advertisement is unforgivable, not only because it will appear dull in an on-line context but also because it means having sacrificed the opportunity to engage the customer actively. Finally, advertisers must remember that advertising in a virtual community, rather than being perceived as a nuisance that interrupts sports events or the flow of a magazine article, may be seen as having intrinsic value. It may be a reason for community membership: for many people, their communities will be places where they know they can find the products they are looking for. This makes placement even more crucial. If a customer is looking for an advertisement, it is all the more important that he or she be able to find it easily.

Marketers who are quick to catch on to the potential of on-line advertising—advertising that is designed to stimulate sales directly and that is placed appropriately in the right context within the right community—stand to improve the effectiveness of their marketing programs overall.

Make use of the new "efficient" pricing

Virtual communities create pricing challenges. Electronic commerce in general may lead markets to become more efficient as community members track down the cheapest prices offered by vendors or put software tools to work to do this for them and put their orders out to bid. As we mentioned in chapter 2, customers will begin to capture some of the economic surplus that suppliers have traditionally been able to claim because of customers' lack of perfect product and pricing information in most markets. Virtual communities make pricing more efficient, as members of consumer or business communities tell each other about excellent deals on offer from a particular supplier.

This has several implications for vendors. Higher-priced vendors are probably the most affected. They must justify their price differential through genuine product advantages and effective communication of these benefits. On the bright side, virtual communities give marketers an opportunity to experiment with pricing. For example, a vendor might learn enough about the needs of a community's members to be able to develop pricing packages that meet the needs of different market segments. Alternatively, a vendor might experiment with different pricing levels at different points in time to test how pricing affects volume. This ties back to the notion of mass customization; one way to tailor a product to customer needs is to test different product features—including price—constantly to establish the optimum for both customer and vendor. Aggressive marketers will use the community to improve the effectiveness of their pricing strategies.

Leverage communities to create true customer loyalty

Customers in many markets are searching for value, not stability; price, not relationship. In the food industry, even marquee brands have found it hard to protect their market share against retailers' competing private label products, which have been developed almost overnight by retail chains such as Sainsbury's in Britain, Loblaw's in Canada, and A&P in the United States. In the wholesale banking industry, "relationship

banking" is being challenged: in some of the more competitive financial markets, banks must win every next piece of business from their
commercial customers. In other industries, price reductions masquer-
ade as loyalty programs, raising suspicions that they are simply shifting
value to customers without discernible long-term benefits for the producers or service providers.

Yet when companies talk about "loyalty," they often unconsciously
have a one-way street in mind—and it goes their way. Companies want
to know in detail about their custom-
ers, gather information about them
assiduously, and sell it on to anyone
willing to pay for it—but get nervous if
customers share information among
themselves about the company and its
products. Companies want customers
to be loyal, but economics determine
their decisions to continue making a
product or to continue selling to a par-
ticular group of customers. Companies want loyalty but have rarely
been able to cultivate one-on-one relationships with their customers,
particularly in consumer markets.

*What you thought
was "loyalty"
was really a
one-way street.*

The lack of one-on-one relationships is not surprising when your
customer base numbers in the millions. But communities might change
the game and help companies develop closer ties to their customers.
Through member profiles and interactions on bulletin boards, communities allow companies to understand their customers better. Through
a combination of bulletin boards sponsored by the company, e-mail
connections back to the company, and on-line events hosted by company representatives, communities also allow companies to interact
personally with customers. And they allow companies to demonstrate
their responsiveness to customers by acting on specific suggestions and
feedback and communicating the impact of these actions back to community members. Admittedly, communities allow a third party—the
community organizer—to step between vendor and customer, but in
many cases such third parties already exist (retailers, for example), and
in others this should encourage many vendors to consider becoming
community organizers themselves.

If loyalty is defined in terms of repeat purchases, or "coming back
for more," communities are a tremendous vehicle for increasing loyalty

to a vendor's products. This is not because vendors will enjoy monopolies in communities. Far from it: as we have already asserted, we believe communities will offer a full range of competing products. Loyalty will be driven by the relationship a supplier develops one-on-one with customers, through customized advertising, two-way sharing of information, and possibly customized products. It will be reinforced by the fact that communities attract enthusiasts, and these enthusiasts will form virtual "fan clubs" around products and suppliers. In addition, assuming a vendor has access to the community's member profiles, it will be alerted sooner than in the off-line world if a customer has stopped purchasing. It will then be able to target marketing efforts at that customer, wooing her back before she has time to accustom herself to a rival product.

Vendors should take advantage of communities not only to improve their understanding of individual key customers but also to build a track record of good service and responsiveness to their needs. The loyalty they create in the process will be based on performance, not brand, but it will serve to build up brand value in the process.

Refocus the sales function on customer management

Across many industries, the heart of the sales function has not changed materially in the past forty years. There continues to be an emphasis on the sales manager as the person pounding the sidewalk, pounding on tables, or pounding on brokers and distributors. The sales manager is by and large not seen as a customer manager. Virtual communities will go some way toward changing that.

In a virtual community, the selling function is shared by several different players. Advertisements can expand to include a selling function. Chat hosts on bulletin boards may become discreet salespeople, pointing members toward areas where they can buy what they are looking for. The community merchandiser may also be arranging special events or promotions (some of which may feature a vendor's best salesperson) to stimulate transactions. If there is any selling left to do in the community, the community members themselves will tout the relative pros and cons of different products to each other. We are not suggesting that salespeople will be made redundant by communities; they will still be needed to sell through physical channels. One or two of the best of them may go on-line to sell products in on-line forums, but, in general, the salesperson's role in the on-line world will be different.

Team up with marketing. The interaction of the sales and marketing function can be difficult. But in a virtual community environment such as the one we have described, where the lines between marketing and selling are blurred, it is important for the two functions to interact seamlessly. Now that advertising takes on a selling role, the sales function should have input into the design of advertising and other on-line marketing efforts, where they can offer insights on what selling tactics might be effective with on-line customers. This interaction should go two ways. The sales function should be willing to get feedback from marketers on sales "pitches" that appear to work in the on-line arena and might have application in the off-line world—and those that don't work.

Emphasize customer management. The detailed customer profiles and tailored marketing programs made possible by the virtual community will call for improvements in a company's ability to manage customer profitability. Tailoring products and advertising to the wrong customers could be an expensive mistake. It will therefore be important for the sales function to be equipped (in terms of skills and analytical tools) to perform this customer management role, assuming it is not performed by the marketing function. This role might include the development of "bidding" strategies aimed at winning the business of certain customers or types of customers when reverse markets materialize and customers do indeed start putting their orders out to bid.

Watch out for new competitors. The advent of virtual communities may lead to the emergence of new competitors. Salespeople need to keep an eye on the virtual marketplace to make sure they know who they are selling against. Communities can change the rules of the game and allow smaller players to turn the tables on larger players. They can also change a company's competitiveness, if, for example, one company offers product descriptions, electronic ordering capabilities, package-delivery tracking, and customer service on-line, while another does not. There is evidence of all four of these activities online today. Salespeople need to keep abreast of these developments, know how to sell against them in the off-line world, respond where appropriate (such as by offering on-line customer service), and keep the marketing function informed about new competitive threats. An aggressive sales force, of course, will take the lead in offering these tools to its key customers.

REINVIGORATING OTHER FUNCTIONS

The virtual community can help to improve the performance of functions other than marketing and sales by offering them a combination of more options, better information, and broader access to people and markets. Some of the functions that stand to benefit most are discussed below.

Strategic planning

Most large corporations develop strategic plans with long time horizons, and many use a scenario-based approach to planning. Virtual communities open up a new range of possible scenarios. Trying at this early stage in the game to develop a radical yet reasonable scenario represents a significant challenge (as we can attest). But playing out the potential business dynamics arising from the successful emergence of virtual communities can be a useful exercise that challenges ingrained notions about a particular industry and its structure. Indeed, it may force major players in an industry to rethink their approach to serving their markets. It may also encourage smaller players to consider ways to expand their market presence by trying to establish a strong competitive position in the new channels created by virtual communities.

In the nearer term, if a business decides to organize a virtual community, its strategic planners must contend with forecasting the economics of the community. Initially, this will be a challenge. The cost structure will be unusual for most companies, and revenues will not only be hard to predict but also, because of the increasing returns dynamics, complex to model. Communicating the challenges, urgency, and payoffs of entering the community organizing business will be all the more difficult because of the possible need for a shift in mindset on the part of top managers, as we described in chapter 7, especially given the relatively long ramp-up period before revenues start to take off. The low up-front investment should mitigate some of these difficulties and might encourage senior managers to endorse the richer set of competitive options that communities can provide. Realistically, the need to understand the potential threats posed by virtual communities may prove to be the most persuasive argument for near-term entry.

Information systems management

If virtual communities become a permanent feature of their business, information systems managers will have a heavier workload. The challenges will principally be on the software rather than the hardware side. While some of the software functions involved in organizing a community are likely to be outsourced, IS managers will still have to understand these functions well enough to know what is important and who has the necessary skills to perform them. Software-related functions will include designing the "look and feel" of the community, creating the information architectures that allow member-generated content to be accessed effectively, and building the systems to capture and manage the member profiles.

IS managers must understand these new, public-network environments and be able to advise senior managers on how to perform the necessary technological balancing act described in chapter 8.

The upside lies in the development of virtual communities designed to meet the needs of IS professionals. As such communities emerge, IS professionals should take advantage of them so as to stay informed about their rapidly changing industry and to enhance the network of peers to whom they can turn for advice on difficult technical issues, new products, and service providers.

Human resource management

The 1990s have kept the human resource manager busy with retrenchments, downsizings, and mergers. Yet, like sales, many core HR functions—such as labor relations, hiring, evaluation and career track management, compensation, and benefits management—have changed little over the past ten or even twenty years. Major corporations by and large still require many of the same skills. This may change in industries where virtual communities emerge in force.

As we have seen, organizing virtual communities requires the creation of some new roles. An HR manager must have a perspective on what these roles are, whether they can be outsourced, or how they can be developed in-house. Community organizing will also demand that existing functions acquire new skills and a new mindset. If larger organizations are to adapt, HR managers must play a role in ensuring that these new skills are understood and acquired. This will mean training existing managers to break out of their mindset and address the opportunities of the technology creatively. It will also mean motivating organizations to accept more uncertainty. In many cases this will be difficult, because most people shy away from technology if they do not understand it—senior managers especially. HR managers alone cannot be held responsible for making sure that corporate cultures adapt to change, but they can help. This will mean making sure that a few of the right people are in powerful enough positions to steer the company in new directions and creating the evaluation and compensation mechanisms to support risk takers. If virtual communities are to be an opportunity as opposed to a threat, the HR manager must understand them conceptually and anticipate them organizationally.

On the recruitment front, communities are providing a new channel for the labor market. There are numerous areas on the Internet where people can post job listings or place their resume. Often these take the form of bulletin boards within a broader site. Cal Law, for example, has an area called Cal Law Legal Classifieds, where California law firms can post position descriptions for attorneys, paralegals, and secretaries. In addition, like IS managers, HR managers across many industries can benefit from the virtual community in terms of its networking potential—in their industry and their profession—and its capacity to help them better understand the labor markets in which they operate.

These observations have focused on how virtual communities might change the way business functions are managed. In the last chapter, we discuss how they might affect the way corporations are managed and the way markets are structured.

10

reshaping
markets and
organizations

Virtual communities hold the power to reshape industries and business organizations. By undermining traditional advantages of scale, they give rise to a new entrepreneurialism that may threaten the hegemony of today's largest corporations. Those who understand, adapt to, and shape the new forces unleashed by this new way of doing business stand to generate considerable wealth. Those who continue to play by the old rules may find themselves destroying value instead.

VIRTUAL COMMUNITIES ARE LIKELY TO SET
in motion a broad range of changes in today's business landscape.
By shifting the emphasis from the producer's perspective to the customer's, communities will reshape market and industry structures. By
evening out information asymmetries, they will help drive the expansion of markets. By making markets more efficient, they'll dissem-
inate information more widely. By opening direct channels of
communication between producers and customers, they'll threaten the
long-term viability of traditional intermediaries. And by giving rise to
a wave of electronic start-ups across a broad spectrum of industries,
they will challenge the established position of some of today's largest
corporations.

VIRTUAL COMMUNITIES REDEFINE MARKETS

Virtual communities redefine markets by expanding demand. They
also redefine markets by focusing on customers rather than on traditional producer-driven notions of "industry."

Expanding demand

In chapter 2 we saw how demand should expand as virtual communities reduce costs. Leaving microeconomics aside, there are other ways
that demand should increase. Electronic networks can cross geopoliti-
cal boundaries, expanding suppliers' reach into new markets. Shopping
sites such as the UK Shopping Mall are starting to add global sections
to give British customers access to overseas markets. However, if this

kind of outreach is to have a material impact on commerce, sellers have to be helped to find buyers. Communities can play an important role in bringing the two parties together.

Communities (as distinct from electronic commerce in general) act as a clear meeting point for individuals or entities with like interests to connect and inform one another about where to find specific suppliers or buyers. They also serve as a meeting point for a critical mass of customers who are thereby put within reach of advertisers.

Communities' effectiveness in bringing together vendors and customers might be particularly high in markets that are inefficient because they are very localized. The food business is dominated by a relatively small number of national and international brands. Countless products are made and distributed at a local level, but they are trapped in the small producer's catch-22: because they can't afford national advertising, they can't generate the volume required to be placed on the shelves of national supermarket chains; if they had the volume, they could of course afford the advertising. Virtual communities can give such small producers national, targeted marketing capability for the price of an on-line ad. Skyline Chili, a favorite among residents of Cincinnati, Ohio, could market itself through a community for people who have spent time as residents of Cincinnati or a community of gourmets interested in trying regional cuisine. Virtual communities could give it broader exposure, although they would not change the economics of nationwide distribution.

Communities may also stimulate demand in people who would not otherwise have thought to purchase a particular item. A gardening supply company might stimulate an interest in gardening among home owners with no prior affinity for it by sponsoring an area in a home and garden community where gardeners talk about their hobby. Conversing with an enthusiastic gardener could pique their interest. In communities, enthusiasts act as natural salespeople. By offering information, they can stimulate interest where it was latent or where it didn't exist before.

Some companies will aggressively embrace the potential of virtual communities to expand their markets. Their challenge will be to decide where they believe latent demand for their products exists and then what communities they should organize or participate in to tap into this potential demand.

Defining markets around customers

Virtual communities force a redefinition of markets around customers in two ways. First, they encourage companies to cross industry lines, driven together by their common need to meet customer needs. We have asserted that the virtual community must have a distinctive focus. We have also discussed how communities need to be managed "organically" and how their growth must respond to the needs of members rather than conforming to the predetermined planning needs of the organizer. Consequently, companies as disparate as Johnson & Johnson, Procter & Gamble, Toys "R" Us, and the New York Hospital/ Cornell Medical Center might find themselves partners in a parenting community.

Second, communities make it possible for different functional areas within a company to give up their singular definitions of a market in favor of one market accurately targeted at potential customers. Communities do this by *becoming* the markets. What do we mean by this? Take a company selling cereals. Its "market" is defined differently by various business functions. The cereal producer might create a "healthy" cereal based on information about certain groups that market researchers have defined as being interested in healthy living. But when the advertising department comes to devise an advertising campaign, it must place advertisements in media that do not correspond exactly to the market seg-

Communities redefine markets by becoming the markets.

ments devised by the marketing and market research functions. Advertising markets are defined in terms of magazine readerships or TV program audiences. Then, as the sales function devises its selling programs, it might think of cereal markets in terms of geographic regions and types of retail outlet, such as supermarkets, drugstores, or warehouse stores. The virtual community can avoid this ambiguity by presenting the producer with one physical set of customers that have already predefined themselves as a group based on similar buying needs and interests. The cereal producer might target a bicycling community, leverage the members' profiles to understand more about their needs, advertise to selected members based on this information, and then sell to this same set of people. This brings an added consistency to market definition and unites each of the company's functions around the same sets of customers.

Companies that embrace the concept of virtual communities as a way of strengthening their ties to customers must decide which communities will offer them the best access to their most attractive customers—and which they should therefore either organize or participate in.

VIRTUAL COMMUNITIES RESHAPE INDUSTRY STRUCTURE

Communities will act as catalysts for structural change in industries. They will do so by reshaping distribution channels and possibly by disintermediating retailers, agents, or distributors. They are also likely to give impetus to a wave of new players in existing industries, some of which will challenge the less innovative of today's largest corporations. As a result, they will oblige many businesses to rethink the basis of their competitive advantage.

Getting organized: Intermediaries should be first

As we saw in chapter 9 in discussing the impact of virtual communities on the selling function, communities have the ability to add to—and possibly displace—existing intermediaries. Over time, a successful travel community will accumulate large numbers of travelers, gather detailed information about their needs and preferences, and establish links to their principal suppliers, including airlines, shipping lines, hotel chains, and rental car agencies. This will position it to displace traditional intermediaries (travel agents), to become an agent, and to take the agency commission for itself.

More ambitiously, in a country with a health care system that has few well-entrenched intermediaries (such as some Western European nations) or in a health care industry that is in the early stages of development (as in many emerging markets), a trusted health care community organizer could play a valued intermediary role. This might include helping doctors understand the efficacy of different pharmaceuticals and medical devices and helping the payor (in many cases the government) to keep track of costs and to assess the cost effectiveness of different treatments. Given the importance of health care to any economy, the value an effective and trusted intermediary could create is potentially enormous, eliminating the need for other intermediaries, helping to identify and promote effective treatments and eliminating ineffective ones.

A virtual community's ability to play an intermediary role in a given industry will depend on a number of factors, such as:

- The extent to which on-line delivery of products substitutes effectively for off-line channels. For example, an automotive dealer provides services before and after a sale that would be hard for a community to replicate.

- The strength of its bargaining position within that industry. The higher the proportion of a market a virtual community accounts for, the greater its chances of being able to negotiate its way into the industry as an intermediary.

- The vulnerability of traditional intermediaries to erosion of their market share. If traditional intermediaries' margins are low and their fixed costs high, a small erosion of that share by a community will have a significant impact on their overall profitability. This will make them fiercer about protecting their market share and more difficult to dislodge in the near term. Newspapers, for example, have a high fixed-cost base. Between 60 percent and 75 percent of the costs of the average paper are fixed, including the cost of editorial content, circulation, advertising sales, operations, distribution, and overhead. Local geographic virtual communities—or communities centered on home- or car-buying—could step in as a new intermediary between sellers, buyers, news gatherers, and news readers. They could offer a more potent form of classified ad (with video clips or direct e-mail connections to sellers), packaged with news clips from the wire services. Even if the communities took only a small portion of readership and advertising away from a newspaper, they could have a significant negative impact on its economics.

Intermediaries' response to the development of virtual communities is likely to be aggressive and preemptive. In fact, as mentioned previously, some intermediaries may be in a good position to become community organizers. It may be easier for them to offer a complete array of competing products and services than it would be for one manufacturer or service provider, who must team up with competitors to offer customers the same degree of choice. In some industries, such as financial services, where a bank acts as both a producer (for example, loan origination) and a distributor (for example, sale of a wide variety of mutual funds), the decision to become a virtual community organizer may be more difficult. As an organizer, would it be content—and would other banks trust it—to offer its own loans in fair competition with those of other banks? One option may eventually be to split production from distribution where that is feasible. In a sense, this was the course pursued by AMR, the parent of American Airlines, when it separated the airline from its reservations service—easySABRE—which is coincidentally playing an aggressive role on-line through its sponsored on-line site, Travelocity, described in chapter 5.

Communities drive a wedge between production and distribution.

These dynamics create clear threats and opportunities across many industries. Aggressive intermediaries will assess how best to protect themselves against the threat of disintermediation and at the same time seize the initiative to organize communities. Producers must assess the long-term nature of their relationship with intermediaries before deciding on their approach to the community business.

Rewarding excellence

Communities will further strengthen companies that demonstrate excellence in management. By making markets more efficient, they will reward companies able to manage their cost structure effectively when market prices come under pressure. By systematizing word of mouth, communities will tend to reward companies that give their customers excellent value. Community members will spread the word about product quality; companies will benefit from satisfied customers' comments to other members of the community and so reinforce the quality part of their value proposition.

To the extent that a smaller company offers a better product or better customer service, it will have a better chance of promoting these strengths in a virtual community than in the off-line world. Its ability to communicate its product message will no longer be a function of its ability to purchase advertising exposure. Certainly, economies of scale may still exist in areas such as physical production and distribution of goods. But large corporations have also enjoyed many scale-related advantages in the areas of marketing and sales, which virtual communities will erode. They will provide cheap and easy access to customers in national and even global markets, thereby undermining some of the advantages that larger companies have enjoyed, such as their ability to get space on the shelves of large retailers, their ability to buy expensive TV advertising, and their global distribution networks. What's more, community organizers may actively promote smaller companies in the belief that as the community struggles to build up a critical mass of subscribers, smaller companies will be more willing partners as vendors than industry leaders.

The leveling of the playing field that virtual communities are likely to bring about suggests that companies—whether large or small—should focus more than ever before on the excellence with which they deliver their value proposition. As we said earlier in reference to the marketing function, product value will win over brand name as never before.

Fostering competition

The economics and organizational requirements of community organizing suggest that many early entrants into the community organizing business will be small ventures run by entrepreneurs. Each of these individuals stands to make millions of dollars in a few years if successful—no matter if the multiples dreamed up by Wall Street are high or low. In isolation, this scenario appears harmless enough: larger corporations might reason that communities will remain a marginal business for the next five years, accounting for only fractional percentages of their total markets.

But just as piranhas reverse the generally accepted principle that the bigger fish eats the smaller fish, so too may virtual communities become a threat to big corporations if they flourish in enough numbers. If more than a handful of communities that touch on a particular industry survive the first two or three years, and if any are successful in wooing significant (albeit small) proportions of that industry's customer base, they pose a long-term threat. The "start small" entrepreneurial nature of the virtual community business may lull the corporate titan into a false sense of security. This may be deepened by the indirect way in which communities grow along vectors; some may seem to have suddenly appeared from nowhere. A toy retailer should be watching out for a demographic parenting community that grows out of a number of local geographic communities: it may soon play host to toy manufacturers selling direct to customers on-line. If the law of increasing returns does in fact apply to the community-organizing business, as we believe, then community growth is likely to accelerate quickly after a slow start. Once on a growth track, communities' smallness is an advantage. They will be faster and more flexible than industry leaders in responding to product feedback. Like MCI in the early days of its battle with AT&T for share of the long-distance market, they will also enjoy the benefit of initially having a small market share that permits them to be more aggressive on price. Who would have given MCI a chance against such a well-entrenched competitor? Yet it was capitalized at more than $15 billion at the time of the takeover bid.

Large companies must beware these "piranha economics." In the near term, say the next two years, the impact of virtual communities will be close to negligible. In the medium term, virtual communities will likely take "nips" out of the economics of these corporations that could weaken their profitability disproportionately. In the longer term, five to ten years from now, these communities might threaten the market position of some of today's industry leaders. This is especially likely in service industries and intermediary industries

Beware "piranha economics."

(such as retailing) that have high fixed costs or a high fixed-asset base, where even small changes in revenue can have a major impact on profitability. Larger corporations should consider how to increase their awareness of these small competitors, whom they might not normally even track, and decide how best to compete against them or possibly partner with them.

Undermining traditional sources of advantage

At an extreme, communities may challenge some of the strategic assumptions on which many of today's larger corporations are built—namely, (1) that capital breeds competitive advantage because it is needed to buy the means of production that in turn yield economies of scale and (2) that high capital requirements act as barriers to entry. Communities do not require large amounts of capital. As we saw in chapter 3, the start-up capital requirements are within the reach of a persuasive entrepreneur with a good business plan. And that capital can yield a high return, given enough time to do so.

Larger corporations will look for ways to respond to communities' successful invasion of their turf, and they might do so by trying to raise capital-intensive barriers to entry. This will not be easy to do, although it's possible that the same technology that allows entrepreneurs to enter the market today with impunity may tomorrow become their Achilles heel. How might this happen? Large corporations might be capable of introducing sophisticated software tools (perhaps some of the overlay technologies described in chapter 8) for managing member profiles or for customizing content—tools that add significant value for vendors, advertisers, or members. It's hard to know at this stage what these might be, but if the value is significant enough, and if the technology is expensive enough to build and operate, size and access to capital would become an advantage again. For this scenario to hold true, you would have to believe that the incremental value created by the technology was significant and that entrepreneurs would be unable to fund the necessary investment. We should add that there is no clear evidence to support such a scenario at the time of writing.

Alternatively, corporations could try to beat start-up organizers at their own game by setting up communities of their own. To do this, they will have to foster an unusually entrepreneurial and creative subculture within their organizations. At the same time, this subculture will have to cooperate with the corporate parent so that the virtual community can benefit from its access to potential members, content assets, and relationships with other vendors.

VIRTUAL COMMUNITIES RESHAPE THE CORPORATION

We have seen how the opportunity to gain better access to customers, and the competitive pressure caused by the successful emergence of virtual communities, may change the way functions are managed within businesses. The virtual community model may also lead to change in the way businesses as a whole are managed. Within businesses, they may improve management effectiveness by speeding up the emergence of "communities of process" that link together cross-functional teams that are focused on the same set of business processes. Within business spheres of influence, the community form may cause the traditional boundaries of the corporation to blur as extended enterprises and corporate partnerships emerge, focusing corporate entities on those functions they perform best while outsourcing the rest.

Communities of practice and process

Traditionally, companies have organized themselves along strictly functional lines, but this "vertical" model is breaking down. Increasingly intense competition, pricing pressures, fast-changing market trends, and the availability of more complex information make it more important than ever for functions to work closely together rather than semi-autonomously.

Many companies have tried to respond to this need by organizing around core processes (such as product development, management of the brand franchise, customer management, and product supply or the supply chain). The trouble is that this requires significant interaction between functions, which many corporate cultures find hard to achieve. For example, the development of new products requires frequent and effective interactions between R&D, marketing, manufacturing, purchasing, and sales. In the past, the answer was to get all the relevant managers together for meetings. In practice this has led to organizational paralysis, as capable managers spend hours in meetings where their contribution could have been limited to minutes.

Applying the principle of the virtual community to this problem by establishing electronic bulletin boards and meeting areas, supplemented by e-mail and even videoconference facilities that allow people to communicate electronically without leaving their desks, could reinforce informal networks that already exist and strengthen integration across organizational divides. These internal corporate communities could take the form of communities of practice, linking members of a particular function (say market research) from around the world, or communities of process, linking team members from different functional areas based in different parts of the country that are involved in executing a core process (such as developing a particular product).

These internal business communities may vary somewhat from the other forms of community we have looked at in the way they meet the needs for interaction. "Transaction needs" are more likely to be met through information exchanges rather than economic ones, for example. But like the virtual communities we have described, communities of practice or process are likely to be organic. In "The Invisible Key to Success," Thomas A. Stewart describes such informal business communities as follows: "Learning happens in groups. . . . Not every group learns. . . . . Groups that learn . . . have special characteristics. They emerge of their own accord. . . . They collaborate directly, use one another as sounding boards, teach each other. You can't create communities like this by fiat, and they are easy to destroy" (*Fortune*, 5 August

Strengthen your company's informal communities by transforming them into virtual communities.

1996, 173). The article goes on to describe how a vice president in an R&D department of NYNEX, a U.S. telephone company, found that by putting individuals from different functional departments into the same room and allowing this kind of community of practice to form (in this case physically, not electronically) without management direction, provisioning of customer data services was cut from seventeen days to three.

Companies that take these lessons to heart, creating the network infrastructure and establishing the culture that allows such communities to form, but without trying to dictate them into existence, will benefit from the natural ingenuity and collaboration of their employees. They will probably end up with happier employees as well.

Accelerating the development of extended enterprises

Private virtual business communities may emerge that tie companies to one another electronically as, together, they create, produce, market, and distribute products. In these networks, traditional boundaries between independent companies may blur, causing the various companies to become one "extended enterprise."

Companies have for some time been moving away from the vertical integration model that at one point led Time, Inc., to own the forests that provided the paper its magazines were printed on. But companies are now moving even closer to a business model that relies on considerable interaction between independently owned companies. Manufacturers are increasingly partnering with their key suppliers, sharing information that once would have been considered proprietary. Competing multinationals such as IBM and Toshiba, Kodak and Fuji are entering into product development agreements even as they compete aggressively in the market for their respective end products. Businesses with large groups of suppliers or distributors can improve decision making by developing private networks that connect them to each other. Wal-Mart is connecting its largest suppliers (such as food and paper product companies) to a network with Wal-Mart at the hub. Products are ordered and inventories managed electronically.

What might the principle of the virtual community add to these networks? These types of network carry information, but they rarely allow for dialog. Adding bulletin boards could allow suppliers and distributors to connect, share ideas, and resolve issues. They would, in a sense, be extended versions of the communities of process just described, building trust across corporations in the same business sphere, as problems are solved jointly.

Stimulating more partnerships

One interesting side effect of virtual communities may be the degree of partnership they stimulate between companies. Some countries' economies are already characterized by a high level of partnering between large corporations—such as the *keiretsu* of Japan and the extensive cross-ownerships and holdings of the German and Italian business worlds. However, it is the exception rather than the rule for companies in other countries, like the United States, to partner extensively with each other. Virtual communities may change that.

It is hard to come up with examples of vendors cooperating with one another on-line today because most businesses have so far chosen to adopt the "corporate Web site" approach. But imagine, for a moment, a community in which many vendors take part. Would the aggregation of these vendors be any different from their appearance together as advertisers in the same magazine or on the same TV show? It certainly will if they are jointly organizing a community, because they will each have access to members (and probably their profiles), and because each company is likely to want a say in how the community is designed. It is hard to imagine groups of competing producers cooperating to organize a community in the near term—it would certainly raise interesting legal issues. It is perhaps easier to imagine groups of competing intermediaries (say retailers or agencies) gathering to organize a community as a preemptive maneuver against the threat of disintermediation.

As vendors interact in the organization of the community, and especially as they begin to understand the needs of the same set of customers, they may begin to find synergies along various dimensions, such as the sharing of purchasing, customer information management, customer service, and product distribution. Alliances or joint ventures might be the result—to the extent permitted by antitrust regulation.

EPILOGUE

Many of today's fortunes are being built from ideas, not physical assets. Many of today's large high-tech corporations—Apple, Hewlett-Packard, Microsoft—were started by one or two individuals high on vision and low on capital. Successful electronic merchants and community organizers may be the next generation of such fast-growth companies. The difference is that these new companies will probably not limit themselves to the high-tech industry. They could spring up in a wide variety of industries and change the landscape of those industries profoundly at the expense of larger, entrenched corporations.

If successful, virtual communities will spawn new industries: community organizing, bulletin board moderating, software design, and community architecture, among others. Mostly entrepreneurial, rarely capital intensive, they may be a partial antidote for the layoffs of the 1980s and 1990s. But the most radical potential impact of the virtual community may well be its impact on the way individuals manage their lives and companies manage themselves. Communities will serve to connect, much like the postage system and telephone before them. But they will go several steps further than the telephone or fax, as they help the individual to seek out and find. Souls in search of relationship, colleagues in search of teamwork, customers in search of products, suppliers in search of markets: the virtual community might have a place for them all.

management agenda

Since it's impossible in the space of a book to do justice to the specifics of how to establish and run almost any kind of business, we've deliberately avoided writing a "how-to" guide for virtual communities. Still, we wanted to try to answer the question, "So what do I do now?" In an attempt to provide some guidance, we've included here a suggested set of next steps, grouped under four categories, to help the senior manager get started in organizing a virtual community. We hope they're helpful.

Step 1: Experience it.

If you haven't already done so, there is no substitute for going on-line and exploring. The examples we've provided throughout the book might give you a starting point; on-line directories can guide you to those areas which interest you most.

Talk to participants in start-ups and to leading-edge on-line players (if not one and the same) to understand the basics and nuances of this business culture and how it may be different from your own.

Step 2: Build a mock funding plan for a "greenfield" competitor.

Identify a target market of key customers and customer segments, factoring in:

- the relative attractiveness of different customers.
- the degree to which they are already on-line.
- the degree to which they might value a community.

Draw up a value proposition:

- Develop a list of products that could be marketed to this customer group.
- Describe aspects of each product that can/cannot be described on-line to current/prospective customers.
- List products that can/cannot be delivered on-line.
- Describe the benefits/drawbacks of a virtual community to your key customers, especially in terms of those needs not being met adequately today.

Estimate the timing of your entry:

- Target the launch of the community.
- Establish membership targets and a schedule for reaching them.

Estimate the economic impact:

- On your business (overall impact; economics relative to specific existing lines of business).
- On key players in your industry (competitors, intermediaries, and so forth).

Step 3: Develop a proposal for senior management.

As in step 2, for your company, plus . . .
Conduct a competitive assessment of the on-line arena:

- Survey moves on-line by major off-line competitors.
- Survey other players emerging on-line that are offering your category of products or targeting your key customers with other products.
- Assess the impact a successful virtual community might have on your customer relationships and market share.

Assess the potential for disintermediation (if you are a producer):

- The likely impact (positive and negative) on service of your key customers.
- The scale of the impact on your economics if the virtual community substitutes for your intermediaries over time.

- The scale of the impact on your economics if an intermediary organizes its own virtual community.

Estimate the impact of disintermediation (if you are an intermediary):

- The likely impact (positive and negative) on your key customers.
- The scale of the impact on your economics if the community substitutes for you and takes X percent of your share.

Propose a way to get into the community organizing business:

- Assess your preparedness to become a community organizer in terms of assets, skills, and mindset (on the part of senior and line management).
- Evaluate the types of community you might consider building.

Describe the endgame; envision the following:

- The types of community to be organized.
- The types of customer need to be met.
- The size of the community (or communities).
- The range of products offered to customers.

Outline a partnering strategy. This would include:

- An assessment of skill/asset gaps relative to goals for member and vendor recruitment.
- Partnership candidates.
- Other factors (for example, locking up unique content, preempting competitors).
- Degree of ownership you are willing to give up, and nonnegotiables.

Financial requirements:

- Cash flows for years one through three.
- Investment required
- Other requirements (for example, rights to content, brands).

Objectives for:

- The first six months.

- Membership over time.
- Revenue, profitability, cash flow over time.

Other:

- Need for organizational linkages/boundaries with parent organization.

Step Four: Build a team to develop an entry strategy.

Draw up an organization to launch and manage the community:

- List the key skills required.
- Identify sources for those skills (internal, external, outsourced).
- Appoint an executive producer.
- Assemble the team.

Develop an initial marketing plan:

- Product design, including features (directories, bulletin boards, and so forth); determine how the four key needs will be addressed.
- List of preliminary target vendors/advertisers.
- Advertising/PR plan (trade associations, other groups, piggybacking of corporate advertising, if any).
- Identification of initial target members (including influencers).
- Decision on revenue sources (for example, decision to charge subscription fees)

Make early technical decisions:

- Internet versus proprietary service, or some combination of the two.
- Technical functions to be outsourced.
- Key technology decisions (payment system, for example).
- Early information architecture (what data will be captured and how).

Decide on a location (not far from other start-ups or from technical services).

further reading

IN DEVELOPING OUR PERSPECTIVE ON THE MATERIAL presented in this book, we have been influenced by a wide variety of published sources as well as our work with clients. In this section, we present a list of core readings on key topics covered in the book from sources that are readily accessible to the senior executive—both in terms of the availability of the material and its lack of technical or academic jargon. For those who want more information, we provide a list of supplementary readings that go into more depth on specific topics.

Core Readings

Arthur, W. Brian. "Increasing Returns and the New World of Business." *Harvard Business Review* 74, no. 4 (July–August 1996): 100–109.

Hagel, John. "Spider versus Spider." *McKinsey Quarterly*, no. 1 (1996): 4–18.

_____, and Toni M. Sacconaghi. "Who Will Benefit from Virtual Information?" *McKinsey Quarterly*, no. 3 (1996): 22–37.

Kelly, Kevin. *Out of Control: The Rise of Neo-Biological Civilization.* Reading, Mass.: Addison-Wesley, 1994.

Michalski, Jerry. "Community, Part I." *Release 1.0*, June 1993, 1–23.

_____. "Community, Part II." *Release 1.0*, July 1993, 1–16.

Rheingold, Howard. *Virtual Community: Homesteading on the Electronic Frontier.* Reading, Mass.: Addison-Wesley, 1993.

Senge, Peter M. *The Fifth Discipline: The Art and Practice of the Learning Organization.* New York: Doubleday, 1990.

Stephenson, Neal. *Snow Crash.* New York: Bantam, 1992.

Supplementary Readings

Arthur, W. Brian. *Increasing Returns and Path Dependence in the Economy.* Ann Arbor: University of Michigan Press, 1994.

Benedikt, Michael, ed. *Cyberspace: First Steps.* Cambridge: MIT Press, 1991.

Boyer, M. Christine. *Cybercities: Visual Perception in the Age of Electronic Communication.* Princeton: Princeton Architectural Press, 1996.

Boyle, James. *Shamans, Software, and Spleens: Law and the Construction of the Information Society.* Cambridge: Harvard University Press, 1996.

Branscomb, Anne Wells. *Who Owns Information: From Privacy to Public Access.* New York: Basic Books, 1994.

Buchanan, James M., and Yong J. Yoon. *The Return to Increasing Returns.* Ann Arbor: University of Michigan Press, 1994.

Davidow, William H., and Michael S. Malone. *The Virtual Corporation: Structuring and Revitalizing the Corporation for the 21st Century.* New York: HarperCollins, 1992.

Dawkins, Richard. *Climbing Mount Improbable.* London: Viking, 1996.

Fine, Gary Alan. *Shared Fantasy: Role Playing Games as Social Worlds.* Chicago: University of Chicago Press, 1983.

Fukuyama, Francis. *Trust: The Social Virtues and the Creation of Prosperity.* New York: Free Press, 1995.

Gelernter, David. *Mirror Worlds.* New York: Oxford University Press, 1991.

Gibson, William. *Neuromancer.* New York: Ace Books, 1984.

Gilder, George. *Microcosm: The Quantum Revolution in Economics and Technology.* New York: Simon and Schuster, 1989.

_____. "Telecosm." Series of articles appearing in *Forbes ASAP,* 1994–96.

Hafner, Katie, and Matthew Lyon. *Where Wizards Stay Up Late: The Origins of the Internet.* New York: Simon and Schuster, 1996.

Herring, Susan, ed. *Computer-Mediated Communication: Linguistic, Social and Cross-Cultural Perspectives.* Amsterdam: John Benjamins, 1996.

Hiltz, Starr Roxanne, and Murray Turoff. *The Network Nation: Human Communications via Computer.* Cambridge: MIT Press, 1993.

Jones, Steven G. *Cybersociety: Computer-Mediated Communication and Community.* Thousand Oaks, Calif.: SAGE Publications, 1995.

Kauffman, Stuart. *At Home in the Universe: The Search for Laws of Self-Organization and Complexity.* New York: Oxford University Press, 1995.

_____. *The Origins of Order: Self-Organization and Selection in Evolution.* New York: Oxford University Press, 1993.

Laurel, Brenda. *Computers as Theatre.* Reading, Mass.: Addison-Wesley, 1992.

Ludlow, Peter, ed. *High Noon on the Electronic Frontier: Conceptual Issues in Cyberspace.* Cambridge: MIT Press, 1996.

Malone, Thomas W., Joanne Yates, and Robert I. Benjamin. "Electronic Markets and Electronic Hierarchies." *Communications of the ACM* 30, no. 6 (1987): 484–497.

Mitchell, William J. *City of Bits: Space, Place, and the Infobahn.* Cambridge: MIT Press, 1995.

Morningstar, Chip, and F. Randall Farmer. "The Lessons of Lucasfilm's Habitat." In *Cyberspace: First Steps,* edited by Michael Benedikt, 273–301. Cambridge: MIT Press, 1991.

Negroponte, Nicholas. *Being Digital.* New York: Alfred A. Knopf, 1995.

Polanyi, Michael. *Personal Knowledge: Towards a Post-Critical Philosophy.* Chicago: University of Chicago Press, 1958.

_____. *The Tacit Dimension.* Gloucester, Mass.: Peter Smith, 1983.

Rayport, Jeffrey F., and John Sviokla. "Exploiting the Virtual Value Chain." *Harvard Business Review* 73, no. 6 (November–December 1995): 75–85.

_____. "Managing in the Marketspace." *Harvard Business Review* 72, no. 6 (November–December 1994): 141–150.

Rothschild, Michael. *Bionomics: The Inevitability of Capitalism.* New York: Henry Holt and Co., 1990.

Saxenian, Annalee. *Regional Advantage: Culture and Competition in Silicon Valey and Route 128.* Cambridge: Harvard University Press, 1994.

Schrage, Michael. *Shared Minds: The New Technologies of Collaboration.* New York: Random House, 1990.

Schuler, Douglas. *New Community Networks: Wired for Change.* Reading, Mass.: Addison-Wesley, 1996.

Sproull, Lee, and Sara Kiesler. *Connections: New Ways of Working in the Networked Organization.* Cambridge: MIT Press, 1991.

Stephenson, Neal. *The Diamond Age.* New York: Bantam, 1995.

Stone, Allucquere Rosanne. *The War of Desire and Technology at the Close of the Mechanical Age.* Cambridge: MIT Press, 1995.

Turkle, Sherry. *Life on the Screen: Identity in the Age of the Internet.* New York: Simon and Schuster, 1995.

index

A&P, 196–197

access to information, 27–31, 108

activity profiles, 146

advantages of scale, 153–154, 203, 211–212

advertising, advertisers, 3–4, 57, 64, 70, 73, 145–146, 167–168, 173
and core communities, 93–94
and member profiles, 50–51
revenue from, 45–46
sales in, 194–196

Agents, Inc., 142, 189–190

Agriculture Online, 24, 121, 122

Amazon.com, 30, 32, 85
and Book Recommendation Contest, 30

American Airlines, 209

American Express, 79, 140

American Medical Association, 19

America Online (AOL), x, 4, 20, 21, 38, 47, 50, 74, 85, 101, 103, 152, 156,
membership of, 61–62
Motley Fool on, 18–19

AMR, 121, 209

Amsterdam Channel, 119

animation, 178

AOL. *See* America Online

apparel industry, 121–122, 125

Apple, 134

assets
members as, 55–62
unique, 75–77

AT&T, 172, 177, 211

authentication, 176

awareness, generating, 137–139, 143–144

banks, banking, 116, 197

barriers to entry, 212
concentration as, 79–80
factor costs and, 78–79
member relationships and, 77–78
unique assets and, 75–77

Biospace, 121

biotech industry, 121

Brand, Stewart, 60

brand names, 127, 139, 194

browsers, 59–60, 87, 106

bulletin boards, ix, 4, 76, 79, 94, 142, 143, 146, 152–153, 168, 178
communication through, 9, 28
generating traffic through, 134, 136–137
hosts of, 159–160

and subcommunities, 144–145
business
    home-operated, 135–136
    on-line, 115–116, 121–123
business communities, x–xi, 214
    evolution of, 85–108
business dynamics approach, 54–55
    loops and, 49–51, 52–53(figs.)
business functions, 212–213
business-to-business contexts,
    22–24, 58
    functional, 122–123
    vertical industries, 121–122

Cal Law, 202
Cancer Forum, 19–20
Catalog Library, 23
Caterpillar, 88
CD Now, 46
CD-ROMs, 144
chat rooms, x, 79, 94, 142, 144, 146,
    152–153, 161, 168, 178, 198
    hosts, 159–160
choice, vendor, 31–32
churn rates, 77, 78, 153
commerce, 5, 9–10, 16, 116–117,
    196
communication protocols, 175
communities, 99, 120
    affiliate, 93–94
    acquisition of, 80–81
    business-to-business, 121–123
    clusters of, 145, 181
    coalitions of, 5
        assumptions about, 99–100
        entry into, 102–103
        organization of, 97–99,
        103–104
        value capture in, 101–102

and commerce, 16, 116–117
concentration of, 79–80
constellations of, 91, 92, 95–97,
    118
    vendors and, 93–94
consumer-focused, 119–121
core and niche, 91, 93–97
defining, 38–39
demographic, 120
enhancing functionality of,
    143–145
evolution of, 155–156
fractal depth of, 117–118
fragmentation of, 86–87, 89
functional, 122
geographic, 119–120
growth options, 70–71
operating costs of, 62–68
potential size of, 114–115
profitability of, 83, 90
sense of, 152–153
shared services of, 98
topical, 120–121
types, 118–123
vertical industry, 121
communities, management of, 14,
    150, 151, 173
    customer service, 162–163,
        198–199
    data needs, 190–191
    human resources, 201–202
    information systems, 200–201
    organic, 155–157
    requirements in, 168–170
    roles in, 157–168
communities, marketing of, 64, 79,
    169, 220
competition, 112, 140–141, 174,
    181, 199

fostering, 210–211
managing for, 217–218
switching and, 147–148
CompuServe, x, 4, 19, 38, 177, 191
Condé Nast Traveler (magazine), 140
consumers, 7–8, 18–19, 47–49. *See also* customers; members, membership
consumer travel community model, 54, 63, 69
cash flow from, 67–68
costs of, 64, 65(figs.), 80
value creation and, 70–72
content, 66, 128, 136, 137, 140, 178
and communication, 9, 27–29
member-generated, 29–31, 147
content attractiveness dynamic loop, 49–50, 52(fig.)
Continuous Relationship Marketing, 22
"cookie" technology, 106
costs, 74
of acquisition, 80–81
as barrier to entry, 79–80
factor, 78–79
and profitability, 62–68
Council of Logistics Management, 122
Counsel Connect Web, 122
critical mass
building, 132–133, 134
for long-term, 125–126
for revenue, 45–46
customers, 8, 12, 25(fig.), 109, 206
choice, 31–32
information on, 105–106
management of, 198–199
and on-line businesses, 115–116
PR from, 192–193

and products, 191–192
purchasing power and, 30–31
relationship with, 127–128
as "segments of one," 187, 189–191
targeting, 217–218
and vendors, 10–11, 13
customer service, 162–163, 169
customization, 50

data collection, 177, 190–191
Delivered with Love, 36
demand, expansion of, 204–205
demographic communities, 120, 126
development, lateral, 102–103
discussion groups, 191–192
disintermediation, 218–219
Disney, 128
distribution capability, 139

Earth's Best Baby Foods, 36
easySABRE, 209
economics, xii
of increasing returns, 41, 42–45
and membership growth, 59–60
near-term, 72–74, 114–118
economies of scale, 210
economies of scope, 80
editors, 161–162, 168–169, 170
Editors' Notification Service, 32
Electronic Mail & Guardian, 119
enterprises, 214–215
entertainment, 21–22
entry points, 14, 113
entry strategies, 108, 131, 220
and coalitions, 102–103
speed in, 134–135
ESPNET, 21, 23, 127, 128, 160, 161
e-World, 134

excellence in management, 209–210
expansion, long-term, 123–126
Experts On Call, 122

"fan clubs," 198
fantasy, 21–22, 142
farmers, 121, 122, 161–162
Farming Weather, 122
Federal Express, 42, 44, 79
feeding, 156
fees, 45, 47, 69–70
Fidelity Investments, 139–140
finances, 18–19, 22, 34, 71, 120
financial analysis, 51, 54
Firefly, 142, 189–190
fractal breadth, 123–124
fractal depth, 117–118, 121
franchises, 154
Friedman, Peter, 160
Fuji, 215
Furlong, Mary, 20

games, 21, 144
Gardner, David, 18–19, 71
Gardner, Tom, 18–19, 71
garment industry, 121–122
gates, in increasing returns model, 132–133
Gates, Bill, 6
geographic communities, 119–120, 123, 124, 125, 126, 153
graphics, 3-D, 5, 178
growth, 14, 132
    assets and, 56–58
    potential for, 83, 90
    requirements of, 152–157

health care, 207–208. See also medicine

hosting services, 90, 103–104, 172–173, 179
hosts, 79, 159–161, 169, 170, 198
Hot New Products, 23
HouseNet, 156
HR. See human resources management
HTML, 175
human resources (HR) management, 201–202

IBEX, 122
IBM, 172, 215
increasing returns model, 135
    assets and, 55–62
    dynamic loops and, 49–55
    economics of, 41, 42–45
    gates in, 132–133
    profitability and, 62–68
Individual, Inc., 122
industries, restructuring, 207–212
infomediaries
    role of, 104–105
    users as, 106–107
    value capture and, 107–108
information, 17, 104, 115
    access to, 27–31
    architecture for, 174–175
    on customers, 105–106
    on members, 13–14
    organization of, 28–29
    sharing, 214–215
information analysts, 165–166
information networks, 138
information systems (IS), 163, 200–201
infrastructure, 5–6
innovation, 163
integration technologies, 177–178

Intel, 175
interest groups, 120–121
interests, consumer, 18–19
intermediaries, 207–209
Internet, 4, 6, 20, 22, 103, 106
    directories, 135–137
    as network platforms, 175,
        176–183
Internet Relay Chat, 178, 183
investment, 136, 200
    barriers to, 75–80
    near-term economics of, 72–74
    personal, 120–121
    and profitability, 63, 66–67
    risks of, 90–91
IRI, 169
IS. *See* information systems
iSKI, 156

journalism, 39

keiretsu, 215
Kinsley, Michael, 29
Kodak, 215

lawyers, 122, 128, 202
Lexis-Nexis, 39, 128
LiveWorld, 160
Loblaw's, 196
loyalty, 50, 61–62, 88–89, 126,
    197–198

macropayment systems, 180
magazines, 122,129
mailing list companies, 8
Main Quad, 183
Mama Ragu, 173
management, 186, 187
    agenda for, 217–220

of business, 212–213
marketing, 11, 122, 186
    changes in, 187–188, 192–199
    and generating traffic, 137–139
    to "segments of one," 189–191
markets, 24, 25(figs.)
    and customers, 206, 217–218
    expansion of, 35–36
    on-line, 5, 116
    participation fees, 69–70
    redefining, 204–207
    reverse, 17–18
MasterCard, 79, 180
MCI, 39,211
media, leveraging, 139
medicine, 40, 121
member loyalty dynamic loop, 50,
    52(fig.)
member profile dynamic loop,
    50–51, 53(fig.)
member profiles, 50–51, 94,
    143–144, 145, 147–148
    and coalitions, 99–100, 101
    trading in, 46–47
members, memberships, 13, 87,
    155, 163
    acquisition of, 159
    aggregating and retaining,
        129–130
    as assets, 55–57, 76
    content and, 9, 29–30, 49–50,
        147
    and core communities, 93–94
    critical mass of, 125–126,
        132–133
    empowerment of, 155
    engaging, 141–143
    evolving role of, 58–62
    growth in, 38–39

and markets, 35–36
purchasing power of, 33–34
relationships of, 77–78
and resources, 10, 148–149
targeting, 26, 61–62
traffic and, 134–141
usage patterns of, 159–164
value to, 13–14
and vendors, 88–89
merchandisers, merchandising,
    166–168, 169, 170, 195
metering technology, 177
Microsoft, 6, 7(fig.), 42, 79, 174,
    175, 177
Microsoft Network, 20
moderators, 94–95
mortgages, 116
Motley Fool, 18–19, 22, 34, 38, 76,
    120, 156, 181, 183
Multi-User Dimensions (MUDs),
    21
Multi-User Dragons. *See* Multi-User
    Dimensions

"natural owners," 113, 128, 155
NetNoir, 156
Netscape, 71, 106, 174
Nets, Inc., 23, 24
network effects, 51
network platforms, 4, 106
    business models, 182–184
    choosing, 175–184
    hybrid, 180–182
newspapers, 119, 208
Nielsen, 169
Novell, 79
NYNEX 214

Online Career Fair, 23

organization
    of information, 28–29
    organic approach, 14–15,
        155–157
organizers, 5, 10, 32–33
ownership, 104, 109, 113, 128

Paint/Coatings Net, 40
parents, 114, 206
Parent Soup, 120, 156, 157
ParentsPlace, 36, 120
partnerships, partnering, 139–141,
    215–216, 219
payment systems, 177
performance measures, 169–170
personal computers (PCs), 5, 106,
    175, 183
Phoenix TeaHouse, 120
Physicians Online, 40, 121
planning, 7, 200, 206
power, 24, 186
    purchasing, 26–27, 30–31
    of vendors, 87–88, 89–90
pricing, 17, 24, 25(figs.), 69–70, 196
privacy, 47, 106
Procter & Gamble, 46
Prodigy, x, 4, 38–39, 177
products, evaluation of, 191–192
profitability, 83, 90
    and operating costs, 62–68
proprietary on-line services,
    178–179, 181, 183
public relations, 192–193
publishing, 29, 39, 144
purchasing, 122, 148–149
purchasing power, 26–27, 30–31,
    33–34

Rainman, 103

Red Dragon Inn, 21, 38
registration fees, 69–70
relationships
    with customers, 71, 127–128
    member, 77–78, 87, 95, 142
    personal, 146–147
research, 190, 191
resources, 9, 127–128, 176
    aggregating, 10, 14
restaurants, 30, 148–149, 205
retail, retailers, 96–97, 102, 196–197
revenues
    dynamics approach and, 49–55
    members as assets and, 55–62
    near-term economics and,
        72–74
    sources of, 45–49, 70, 73
Russia Alive!, 119

Sainsbury's, 196
sales, 186
    and advertising, 194–196
    and customer management,
        198–199
    strategies for, 187–199
satisfaction, member, 163
scale, advantages and benefits of,
    153–154, 203, 210
scalability, 152–154
seeding, 156
"segments of one," 187
    marketing to, 189–191
SeniorNet, 20–21, 183
SeniorNet Learning Center, 21
seniors, 20–21, 120, 125
shareholders, 68
shopping, 39, 204–205
"shovel ware," 28

Silicon Investor, 121, 153
skills, 79, 108
    management requirements,
        157–168
    organizational, 128–130
Skyline Chili, 205
Slate, 29
Software Support Professionals
    Association, 19
Sony Walkman, 156
South Bend Tribune (newspaper),
    119
sports, 21, 23, 115
SportsZone, 128
standards, technological, 177, 180,
    181
Stock Talk, 153
streaming technology, 178
subcommunities, 93, 117, 157
    advantages of scale in, 153–154
    evolution of, 155–156
    formation of, 124, 125, 144–145
    and sense of community,
        152–153
subscribers, 47
Successful Farming (magazine), 122
supply, 24
Surplus Equipment Service, 23
sysop (systems operator), 159, 160,
    168, 169, 170

talent, 79
Talk City, 183
TCP/IP, 175, 177
technology
    architecture, 164, 174–175, 179,
        183
    commercial activities and,
        177–178

competing business models, 175–176
metering, 177
proprietary, 178–179
standards, 180, 181
streaming, 178
technology choices, 172
technology strategy, 173–175
text description languages, 175
Thrive, 156
Time, Inc., 214
Time-Warner, 39
topical communities, 120–121, 126
Toshiba, 215
Total New York, 119, 162
track records, 78
traffic, 132–133
concentrating, 141–146
generating, 134–141
locking in, 146–149
transaction offerings dynamic loop, 51, 53(fig.)
transaction profiles, 46–47
transactions, 22–23, 51, 57, 95, 167, 177, 213–214
shares of, 68–70
travel agencies, 69
Travel & Leisure (magazine), 48, 140
travel community, 29, 47–48, 80, 92(fig.), 117, 121, 124, 140, 164, 167
value creation in, 70–72
Travelocity, 121, 209

UK Shopping Mall, 204–205
uncertainty, 7, 43
University of San Francisco, 20
UPS, 79

usage rates and patterns, 5, 60, 141–142, 147–148, 169
member, 159–164
USA Today, 47
USENET, 178

valuation, traditional, 51, 54
value, 57, 62, 141, 190, 194, 218
adding, 11, 105
creation of, 12–13, 68–72, 85–86, 104, 113, 119–120
extracting, 145–146, 164–168
to members, 13–14
of on-line business, 115–116
value capture, 85
in coalitions, 101–102
in constellations, 95–97
in infomediaries, 107–108
vendor profiles, 100
vendors, 1, 13, 17, 25(figs.), 37–38, 57, 146, 165, 177
benefits to, 7–8, 10–12
choice of, 31–32
cooperation among, 215–216
and core and niche communities, 93–94, 96–97
infomediaries and, 107, 108
and loyalty, 197–198
and member profiles, 143–144
power of, 87–88, 89–90
and virtual villages, 88–89
vertical industries, 121–122, 213
virtual communities. See communities
Virtual Garment Center, 40, 121–122
virtual villages, 91
characteristics of, 86–87

vendors and, 87–90
Virtual Vineyards, 22
Visa, 79, 180

Wal-Mart, 215
Web sites, 114
Webzines, 129
weeding, 156, 157
Well, The, ix, 4, 5, 47, 60
Well Engaged, 183
wholesalers, 102
wine, 22
World Wide Web, 3, 4, 39, 178

Zagat's guides, 30
Zima Web, 173

about the authors

JOHN HAGEL III is a principal at the Silicon Valley office of McKinsey & Company, Inc., and leader of McKinsey's Interactive Multimedia Practice. His work is primarily with clients in the electronics, telecommunications, and media industries, with a focus on strategic management and performance improvement. Prior to joining McKinsey, he served as senior vice president for strategic planning at Atari; as president of Sequoia Group, a systems house selling turnkey computer systems to physicians; and as a consultant with the Boston Consulting Group. Mr. Hagel is the author of legal and business books and articles.

ARTHUR G. ARMSTRONG is a manager at the New York office of McKinsey & Company, Inc. His work has primarily been with clients in the telecommunications, media, and consumer goods industries, with a focus on organization and performance improvement.

Mr. Hagel and Mr. Armstrong have served clients together and have co-authored articles on the topic of virtual communities for *The McKinsey Quarterly* and the *Harvard Business Review*.